**Editors**

Peter Johnson is the author of seven books on yachting subjects. For more than six years he has contributed the 'In the Offing' column in *Yachting World*. He has been sailing and racing actively for thirty-three years and has owned around a dozen different boats. He serves on the ORC and is closely involved with the organization of international yachting.

Robert Humphreys became editor of the offshore section of *Yachts and Yachting* after taking an honours degree in industrial design. He is now a yacht designer, rating consultant and freelance writer mainly on offshore racing. Recently he designed, built and campaigned his own Quarter Tonner.

Roger Marshall is a designer with Sparkman and Stephens, New York. He is also a freelance writer whose work appears regularly in *Sail* as well as magazines in Australia, England and Japan. Before moving to the USA he studied yacht design at Southampton College, England. He has crewed on many top flight racing yachts, including being a regular hand on *Morning Cloud*.

# OFFSHORE
# MANUAL
## INTERNATIONAL

Edited by **Peter Johnson**

With **Robert Humphreys (Europe)**
**Roger Marshall (U.S.A.)**

Illustrated by **Peter Milne**

*DODD, MEAD & COMPANY · NEW YORK*

Printed in Great Britain

# Acknowledgements

Much of this book follows from the deliberations, minutes and publications of the Offshore Racing Council. Acknowledgement is made to its members. In return for their assistance, sometimes specific, sometimes unwitting, the pages which follow should clarify their intentions for offshore owners, crews and race organizers.

There is much additional material beyond the orbit of the ORC and thanks are due for helping with this and for other assistance in preparation to Mark Baxter; Arthur Giolitto, Marine Division, US Customs; Ian Godfrey, Lewmar Marine; Bernard Hayman, Editor *Yachting World*; Caroline Johnson; Bruce McPherson and Christopher Wick, Sparkman and Stephens; S. Zillwood Milledge; Elizabeth Moncrieff; Ian Nicholls, Barient Winches; Mary Pera; Lt-Cmdr Clinton H. Smoke Jr, US Coast Guard; R. F. Wilson, Bridon Fibres and Plastics and to Dr. Jonathan Rogers, ocean racing man and doctor for the chapter on medicine. The staffs of the Royal Ocean Racing Club and United States Yacht Racing Union have also been most helpful.

Though the editors have tried to interpret ORC policy, any explanation given should not be taken as the only or final word and the latest information on the details of the rating rule, special regulations and so on should be sought through official channels. Nor can any responsibility be accepted for errors or omissions. Wherever possible, the reader is guided to original or current sources.

# Contents

Both metric and English systems of dimensions have been used in this book. The units selected are those which best aid comprehension for the English speaking reader in any particular topic.

# 1. Organizations and events

Every country in the world, where there is any form of organized sailing, has a national yachting authority. Such authorities are entitled to full membership of the *International Yacht Racing Union* (IYRU), whose object is 'the promotion of the sport of amateur yacht racing throughout the world . . .'. The IYRU states in its constitution that it is responsible for two things: (1) rules for racing and (2) rules for international yacht classes which it recognizes. The Union does not, in this sense, recognize offshore boats and these are controlled by the *Offshore Racing Council* (ORC).

The same national authorities are recognized by the ORC, but only those with offshore fleets belong to it. Delegates are restricted in numbers and sometimes act for several countries. There are also two IYRU delegates. The ORC was formed to look after the International Offshore Rule (IOR) but its activities have spread. Fig 1 shows its sub-committees.

The roles of the main sub-committees are as follows:
*International Technical Committee* (ITC) makes recommendations to the Council on rule changes and actually drafts the 'law' for the international offshore rule. It is a small group—maximum seven persons.

*Measurement committee* is where measurers bring practical problems and anomalies which have arisen. Often the resulting decisions are passed to the ITC for insertion in the rule.

*Time Allowance Systems Committee* is concerned with suitable time allowance systems for use with IOR ratings. (see Chapter 17).

*Level Rating Classes Committee* provides the rules for the Ton classes which race to rating limits without time allowances. (See Chapter 16.)

*Special Regulations Committee* makes recommendations to the Council on the special regulations for safety and equipment for IOR yachts and drafts the wording for these rules. (See Chapter 6.)

The Council consists of a chairman and two deputy chairmen and members from countries or groups of countries as follows (the chairmen are included in these numbers, and so are representative members). Australia and New Zealand (1), Benelux (1), Brazil (1), Canada (1), Germany (1), France (1), Greece (1), Italy and Yugoslavia (1), Spain and Portugal (1), Japan (1), South America (except Brazil) (1), Scandinavia (1), United Kingdom and Ireland (3), United States (4), IYRU (2).

**How individuals or clubs get their**

## organization

views or proposals before the international authority for offshore racing boats.

The ORC and its committees cannot provide what sailors want unless there is communication from owners and crews. Resolutions for the ORC have to be submitted four weeks before the council meeting. This is at least annual, usually in early November. National authorities should have some filtering system to deal with the points raised, which can then be rejected, or amended, or go forward as they stand as resolutions to the international body. (Fig 2.)

In Britain this filtering body is the Technical Committee of the RORC administered by the national rating office. Individuals should get their clubs to send resolutions to the technical committee prior to ORC meetings. In the USA clubs should send their resolutions to the National Offshore Council via USYRU which acts as a filtering body.

**ORC Working**
To expedite decisions the ORC secretary sends incoming resolutions to the appropriate committee (rule changes to ITC, One Ton Cup problems to Level Rating, Classes etc.). When the resolution is called in the council, the committee chairman can give his considered recommendations. If the result is positive the council can give immediate ratification and the new ruling, in whatever field, is published and sent to all national authorities. Thence it goes, by arrangements in each country, back to owners and crews.

**Another route for tackling the ORC**
There are two IYRU representatives on the council. National authorities may raise points from their own countries in IYRU meetings. These can subsequently

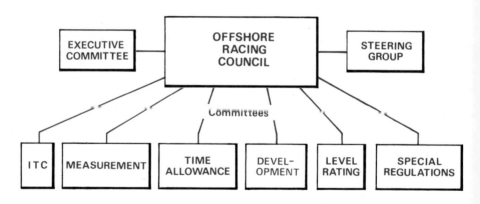

Fig 1. Committee structure of the Offshore Racing Council. In the Council itself there are 24 members representing 14 countries (or groups of countries) and the IYRU.

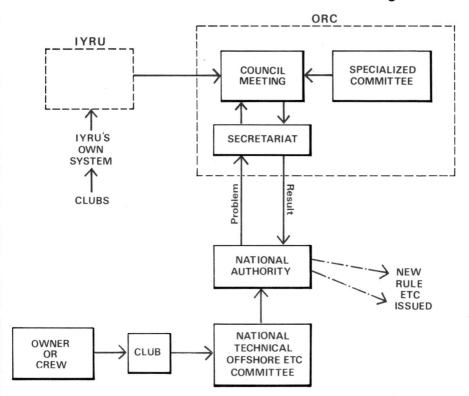

*Fig 2. How complaints and suggestions from the ordinary yachtsman reach the Council and the results (if any) are promulgated.*

be submitted to the council from the IYRU, but are bound to be diluted on the way. The IYRU is unlikely to be interested in minor technical points, but more on matters such as amateurism, new classes and policy affecting racing between countries.

**Chief Measurer's instructions**
Between ORC meetings, the ORC Chief Measurer (who is Chairman of the Measurement Committee) can issue instructions on rating and measurement. This enables so-called loopholes or measuring queries and anomalies to be dealt with instantly. Such instructions are used sparingly and must be ratified, amended or cancelled at the next regular ORC meeting. Instructions are sent from the ORC office to national authorities.

11

# organization

*Fig 3. A typical instruction as issued by the chief measurer between ORC meetings.*

## Useful publications issued periodically by the ORC

The main publication is the *International Offshore Rule Mark III,* with amendments. Administrative publications include *Constitution, Council and Committee members names and addresses.* Regulations issued include *Rules for Level Rating Classes (World Championship)* and *Special Regulations.* (Both issued at the beginning of each year).

## Position of independent clubs and organizations

There is no international co-ordination or authorization for offshore events. Anyone can announce (unless some edict within his own country prevents this) that he is going to hold a yacht race and that it will be run on IOR rating or any other system. In practice, regular races only become established under the auspices of well organized clubs with suitable sailing water. However each club (or association or organization: from now on the word 'club' will be used to indicate the organizing unit for a race) has to announce and then promote its own event.

The authority of the club derives from IYRU racing rule I, 'General authority of race committee'. The club sets up a *race committee* as described in this rule and this decides on the rules to be used and any rules of its own.

The race committee must begin by issuing a 'Notice of Race': the contents of this are listed in IYRU rule 2. Additional notices to IYRU rule 2, for offshore events are:

Maximum and minimum ratings in the race and/or how classes are to be subdivided by rating.

Any other criteria for high or low limits (e.g. LOA or 'L').

Whether any particular time allowance is to be used (this is not essential information at this stage).

Where and when sailing instructions will be available.

Where and when yachts must be presented for inspection and measurement checks (if applicable). Moorings and harbour arrangements.

## Fixtures

Neither the ORC nor any other body can therefore supply a world wide fixture list for offshore boats. National authorities may have co-ordinated lists, but in the bigger countries these are seldom complete. The IYRU has a fixture card, but this is not comprehensive for offshore boats. Yachtsmen are therefore best advised to write to each club concerned for its program. National authorities can be contacted from abroad and may be able to give names of main racing clubs.

**National authorities** (English speaking)

The Australian Yachting Federation
J. A. L. Shaw, The Australian Yachting Federation, 33 Peel Street, Milson's Point, N.S.W. 2061, Australia.

Bahamas
Bahamas Yachting Association, P.O. Box N. 1216, Nassau, Bahamas.

Barbados
The Secretary, Barbados Yachting Association, P. O. Box 40, Bridgetown, Barbados.

Bermuda Yachting Association
Charles W. Kempe, Bermuda Yachting Association, P.O. Box 463, Hamilton, Bermuda.

Canadian Yachting Association
T. L. Phillips, Executive Secretary, Canadian Yachting Association, 333 River Road (11th Floor), Vanier, Ottawa, KIL 8B9, Ontario, Canada.

Hong Kong Yachting Association
P. J. Gamble, Hon. Secretary, Hong Kong Yachting Association, Kellett Island, Hong Kong.

Jamaica Y.A.
The Secretary, Jamaican Yachting Association, c/o Royal Jamaica Yacht Club, Palisadoes Airport P.A., Jamaica W.I.

Irish Yachting Association
The Secretary General, Irish Yachting Association, 87 Upper George's Street, Dun Laoghaire, Co. Dublin, Republic of Ireland. Phone: 800239

New Zealand Yachting Federation
Secretary, New Zealand Yachting Federation, P.O. Box 62103, Auckland, New Zealand.

South African Yacht Racing Association
The Secretary, South African Yacht Racing Association, Private Bag 1, Saxonwold, South Africa. Phone: 42-6977.

## organization

Royal Yachting Association (Racing Manager)
    Victoria Way, Woking, Surrey GU21 1EQ, England. Phone: 048-62 5020.
United States Yacht Racing Union (Director, Offshore Activities)
    P.O. Box 209, Newport, RI 02840, USA. Phone: (401) 849-5202.
US Virgin Islands
    Rudy Thompson, President, Yacht Racing Association of the Virgin Islands, 33 Raadets Gade, St. Thomas, Virgin Islands.

*Principal clubs in Great Britain giving events for offshore boats* (Fig 4)
Royal Ocean Racing Club
    20 St. James's Place, London SW1A 1NN:
Races over 200 miles from British ports and other places.

Royal Naval Sailing Assn:
Round the world race every fourth year

British Level Rating Assn:
For the Ton Cup classes including national championships

Junior Offshore Group:
For IOR yachts under 23 ft rating

Solent Cruising and Racing Assn:
Co-ordinates passage races in the area run by member clubs

South West Offshore Assn:
Co-ordinates passage races in the area run by member clubs

Bristol Channel Yachting Conference:

Co-ordinates passage races in the area run by member clubs

Irish Sea Offshore Racing Assn:
Co-ordinates passage races in the area run by member clubs

Clyde Cruising Club:
Passage races in the west of Scotland

North East Cruiser Racing Assn:
Co-ordinates passage races in the area run by member clubs

East Anglican Offshore Racing Assn:
Co-ordinates passage races in the area run by member clubs

Royal Western Yacht Club of England:
International single-handed and two-man events

RORC

RNSA

14

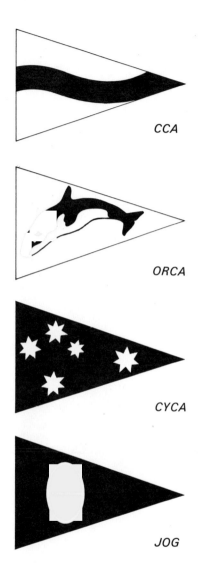

*Principal offshore organizations in Australia*
Cruising Yacht Club of Australia
Middle Harbour Yacht Club

*Principal US organizations holding offshore events*
Offshore Racing Club of America
P.O. Box 14
Rowayton, Connecticut 06853

Promotes offshore racing in the US as well as international competition

New York Yacht Club
37 West 44 Street
New York, New York 10036

New York Yacht Club cruise held in August each year; Annapolis–Newport Race every odd numbered year in June

Cruising Club of America

Co-ordinates passage races on east coast of US; Newport–Bermuda Race every even numbered year in June

St. Petersburg Yacht Club
11 Central Avenue
St. Petersburg, Florida 33701

Southern Ocean Racing Conference races every year in February (St. Petersburg–Anclote Key; St. Petersburg–Ft. Lauderdale; Ocean Triangle; Lipton Cup; Miami–Nassau; Nassau Cup)

*Fig 4. Burgees of some offshore clubs and organizations.*

## organization

*US offshore associations for particular areas and their major events*
(For further information about a race, contact the secretary of the sponsoring association, current names and addresses can be obtained from USYRU. The races listed are held annually unless otherwise specified.)

Yacht Racing Union of Massachusetts Bay

Marblehead—Halifax Race (early July)

Yacht Racing Association of Long Island Sound

Vineyard Race (August/September)
Block Island Race (late May

Yacht Racing Association of San Francisco Bay

San Francisco—Santa Barbara (June)
San Francisco—Newport Beach (September)

Southern California Yachting Association

Tahiti Race (June)
Transpac Race (early July odd numbered years)
Manzanillo Race (February even numbered years)
Mazatlan Race (November even numbered years)
Puerto Vallarta Race (February odd numbered years)
La Paz Race (November odd numbered years)

Texas Yachting Association

Galveston—Veracruz Race (June)

South Atlantic Yacht Racing Association

Charleston Race (down in November, up in March)

Lake Michigan Yachting Association

Trans-Superior Race (August)
Chicago—Mackinac Race (July)
Port Huron—Mackinac Race (July)

Detroit River Yachting Association

Lake Erie Race (July)

Lake Yachting Association

Lake Ontario International Race (August)

Pacific International Yachting Association

Swiftsure Classic (late May)
Victoria–Maui Race (July)

Florida Sailing Association

Miami–Montego Bay Race (early March)
Miami–Kingston Race (March)
St. Pete-Isla Mujeres Race (May)

Hawaii Yacht Racing Association

Around Hawaii Race (mid August odd numbered years)

**Traditional Events**
Bermuda race and Onion Patch team races. Newport, RI—Bermuda 625 miles. Every even numbered year in June. Apply to Cruising Club of America.

Fastnet race and Admiral's Cup team races. English Channel and western approaches. Every odd numbered year in August. Apply to Royal Ocean Racing Club.

Sydney–Hobart race. Every year on December 26. Southern Cross team races on alternate years. Apply Cruising Yacht Club of Australia.

Trans-Pacific race. Los Angeles–Honolulu. Every odd numbered year.

Rio Circuit. Individual and team races from Rio de Janeiro. Each October. Apply to A.B.V.O., Rio de Janeiro, Brazil.

Round Gotland race. July. From Denmark, Norway, Sweden in turn. Enquire Swedish national authority.

*Badge of the Offshore Racing Council*

17

# 2. The laws of offshore racing

Pages of laws govern an offshore yacht taking part in a race. Some of these are in constant use by skipper and crew (right of way, for instance), some only come into effect when certain events take place (rounding a mark, man overboard), some are of application prior to the start (sail numbers, equipment lists), some after the finish (declarations) and some are only directly used by the organizers (time allowance). Sadly, rules grow with the complexity of sport and yachtsmen have to face up to both knowing more rules and where to refer to others, as they increase.

One way to remember the extent of all these rules is to consider them as *vertical* and *horizontal*. The vertical list of rules consists of those issued:

Internationally
Nationally
Regionally (association, group of clubs etc)
At club level or by the organizers of the race or series

In this vertical list each one can invoke the authority of the set of rules above it, or at club level reference can (or should be) made to all or parts of the higher sets of rules. An example of this is on page 21.

The horizontal set of rules refer to different areas of racing. They are specifically: Racing rules, rules of measure-ment and rating, time allowance systems, emergency and equipment rules, admini-strative rules, sailing and course instruc-tions. Fig 5 shows the structure of rules, with examples. The actual rules vary everywhere in the world except that IYRU rules (though with exceptions specified) are always used, the IYRU being the ultimate authority for amateur yacht racing.

Here are some points about types of rule (using the horizontal list and moving vertically through it). Most of these are further expanded on later in this book.

## Racing rules

The IYRU establishes its position under rule 3 of its constitution: 'The Union is the sole authority responsible for the establishment and amendment of rules for international yacht racing'. Presumably this means 'rules for yachts when racing anywhere in the world'. In practice the rules are the only ones used.

The rules are published by the IYRU, as *The 1977 Yacht Racing Rules*.

Under a 1969 bye-law the rules are only amended once every four years, just after each Olympic Games. So there will be new rules dated 1981, 1985 etc. Most countries reprint the rules in their own languages. English is the original.

There were numerous changes in 1977

18

and these should be known by anyone used to the previous rules. There are IYRU rules concerning team racing, protests and the use of an international jury. These are to be found in *The International Yacht Racing Union Year Book*, for the current year.

International offshore events frequently have an international jury. This is not just a collection of people from different countries. It is specifically constituted as laid down under *Terms of Reference of an international jury under racing rule 77.5.*

On *national level* the IYRU rules are in places added to by a national authority. These will be in *the national publication* of the IYRU rules, so in practice have the same source. (For UK, RYA 1/77, for USA 'IYRU racing rules' from USYRU).

When racing in foreign waters, a yacht will invariably be obliged to comply with the national prescriptions to IYRU rules. There is a danger here that the skipper will only be referring to the IYRU rules published in his own language in his own country. But he should obtain the IYRU rules as published in the country in which he is racing. However, race committees should avoid him having to do this by reprinting the national prescriptions on the race instructions. The Ton Cup events waive national prescriptions, but the legality of this is dubious. Printing such prescriptions on the race instructions would, of course, restore the position.

On *regional level* there is often a set of *standing instructions* which apply throughout a season. Most of these may be administrative, but they may state such remarks as 'The bar buoy shall be considered a mark of every course and must always be passed on the seaward side'.

On *race organizers'* (club) level come all the *sailing instructions* and indeed the contents of these are listed in IYRU racing rule 3. That rule states 'These (IYRU) rules shall be supplemented by written sailing instructions which shall rank as rules and may alter a rule by specific reference to it'. Exceptions follow. Note race organizers can abolish the right of appeal against protest but must say so in advance: some national authorities insist on specific permission for such procedure.

Changes in sailing instructions have to be given, 'in writing not later than the warning signal of her class'. 'Oral instructions shall not be given, except in accordance with procedure specifically set out in the sailing instructions.'

## Rules of rating, measurement and time allowances

At *international level*, the measurement rule is *International Offshore Rule IOR Mark III*. The source is the Offshore Racing Council, London, (or obtainable from national authorities as ORC publication or translations) and it is a book of about 60 pages. Amendment pages are issued annually in about January. *IOR Mark IIIA* is included in IOR Mark III and is applicable to certain yachts by reason of their age. (See page 155.)

*Chief Measurers Instructions* are issued from time to time by the ORC. These are to 'plug gaps' usually on minor measurement and rating matters; as soon as possible they are incorporated into the regular rules.

For measuring sails under the IOR, the IYRU sail measurement rules are used, except where otherwise stated in the IOR itself. These rules are to be found in *The*

| "VERTICAL" | Racing | "HORIZONTAL" Rating & measurement | Safety | Administrative |
|---|---|---|---|---|
| **International** | IYRU Racing rules (gives authority to all rules) | IOR Mark III<br><br>IYRU sail measurement | ORC special regs | For level rating classes, 'Green Book', rules |
| **National** | National authority prescriptions | A national time allowance system | Particular life-jacket specification | National sail numbering system |
| **Regional** | Standing instructions about buoys, restricted areas | Possible own handicap system | Extra safety rules | |
| **Race organizers (club)** | Sailing instructions for the race | Possibly own handicap system<br>Age allowances | Extra equipment or exceptions to above | Class divisions<br>Reporting retirements<br>Docking.<br>Protest and jury arrangements |

*Fig 5. Rules for the offshore boat set out in 'horizontal' and 'vertical' form.*

*Measurement Instructions of the International Yacht Racing Union, Section III, Sail Measurement* and *Section IV Sail Area Measurement.*

At *national level* may be found time allowance systems. There is no internationally agreed time allowance system. The most important national time allowance system is entitled *Time Allowance Tables*, issued by the United States Yacht Racing Union. *Booklet A* is decimal hours for tenths of a foot of rating. *Booklet B* (this is bulky) is decimal hours for hundredths of a foot of rating. The USYRU time allowance system is very widely used throughout America and elsewhere when time-on-distance allowances are in operation.

Time allowances not linked to the IOR may be found nationally. In UK the *Portsmouth Yardstick Scheme for Cruisers* is to be found in RYA booklet YR2. 'Yardsticks' and 'Numbers' under the scheme are listed for most standard cruisers.

At *regional level* (or by nationwide associations, e.g. MORC) may be found measurement, rating and time allowance systems other than IOR or time allowance systems used with IOR.

At *club* level the same remarks apply, but outside America this is normally where a time allowance system is originated (e.g. *RORC, TMF formula* to be found in the annual program of races issued by that club). Lists of TMF against every IOR rating are published by the RORC. Age allowances in the form of percentages applied when working out the corrected time are issued at club level.

## Emergency equipment and safety rules

The *international* rules are the Offshore *Rating Council Special Regulations governing minimum equipment and accommodation standards* (published annually by the ORC).

At *national* level, particular countries may have government, Coast Guard etc, safety rules which are invoked by race organizers.

*Race organizers* will specify what safety rules (e.g. ORC or their own or a combination of both with exceptions and additions) are to be used.

## Administrative Rules

At *international* level, these are most likely to be those in the *Level Rating classes* 'green' book (published annually by the ORC); for instance, numbers of crew, scoring systems. Other offshore events are not established at international level. During level rating races the green book is the original point of reference, but is open to overriding by the organizers. Class Divisions (I to VIII) are recommended internationally (but not used in USA).

At *national* level, administrative rules will include sail numbers allocated by the national authority.

*Regional, nationwide associations and clubs* will issue administrative rules of a number of complexions dealing with a race or series. These could include class divisions, class flags, arrangements for issuing course changes, declarations, arrangements for protests, reporting of retirements, reporting by radio during race, procedure if a mark is not seen, restrictions on hauling, time limits for finishing. Docking arrangements and social program for an event would also be issued at this level.

## Extracts from sample sailing instructions and notes

Sailing Instructions

'Races will be sailed under the racing rules of the IYRU, the prescriptions of the national authority, the rules of the 1977 Big Bay points series and these sailing instructions'.

This essentially invokes the *racing rules,* although *administrative* ones may become included in this statement.

'Eligibility—Yachts must have a valid IOR Mark III rating certificate and must conform to the ORC special regulations (January 1977) and the standing emergency rules of the Big Bay points series. The minimum eligible rating is 21·0 feet.'

This invokes international rating and safety rules and regional safety rules. Race organizer's safety rules can appear individually later in the sailing instructions.

'Time allowances will be those of the United States Yacht Racing Union. Big Bay Association 1977 age allowances will be in force.'

This invokes the national time allowance system and adds the race organizers amendment to it.

'Class flags must be flown from the backstay for the duration of the race. Class divisions are shown in the entry list.'

'All yachts shall take their own times of

# offshore laws

finish and make them available to the race committee, if so required.'

'The time limit for the race is 2000 clock time in accordance with IYRU Rule 10'.

These are all typical administrative rules which vary in every race. Others might concern local by-laws for shipping, arrangements for alteration to courses, procedure (under IYRU rule 9.1) when marks go missing, recalls, declarations, postponements, protests, prizes, publication of results. Here are two possible administrative rules of a navigational sort. 'Between 2030 and 0545 navigation lights shall be lit, IYRU rules 36 to 43 will cease to be applicable and will be replaced by Section II (conduct of vessels in sight of one another) of the International Regulations for Preventing Collision at Sea.'

'If a mark is not seen the onus will fall upon the competitor to provide satisfactory evidence that the mark has been passed correctly, failing which the yacht may be disqualified.'

Some people are only concerned (unwisely) with the 'bare bones' of the sailing instructions. These are the start line, time of start, starting signals, course and finish. The authority for these are IYRU rules 3.2, 4, 6 and 7.

'The start line is formed by joining a white flag on the committee boat to blue flag on a circular orange buoy with the letters DM thereon, Cross the line from north to south.'

'Course. Leave Black Rock beacon to port, Winkle light ship to port, Bay Bar buoy to starboard thence to the finish.'

Other details include description and how to cross finish line and procedure for doing so at night.

**Extracts from the rules for sail measurement and for an international jury, shown by kind permission of the IYRU.**

## SECTION III—SAIL MEASUREMENT

### 1. General

(1) Sails shall be measured in a dry state laid on a flat surface with just sufficient tension to remove wrinkles across the line of the measurement being taken.

(2) Sails shall be flexible, soft and capable of being easily stowed. The body of the sail shall be so constructed that it may be folded flat in any direction, other than in way of windows and corner stiffening as defined below, without cracking or otherwise permanently damaging the sail or its reinforcement. Reinforcement of any fabric having the effect of stiffening the sail is permitted only with a distance from each corner of 150 mm plus 3% of the length of the luff of the sail. Other reinforcement, as a continuation of corner stiffening or elsewhere, comprising not more than two additional layers of material having the same weight as the body of the sail, is permitted provided that it can be folded as described above and is not stiffened by the addition of bonding agents, close stitching, or otherwise. Glued seams shall not be considered as stiffening provided that they can be folded as described above. Normal tabling at the edges of the sail is permitted provided that it is not stiffened.

A spinnaker may have reinforcement of any fabric near its centre for attaching a recovery line.

(3) The term 'sail' shall be taken to

include the headboard, tabling, bolt and foot ropes (or tapes). It shall not include cringles which are wholly outside the sail.

(4) Where, under the class rules, a window is permitted, or not specifically prohibited, then the area of the transparent material of such window shall not exceed 0·3 m² and shall not be placed closer to the luff, leech or foot than 150 mm or 5% of the length of the foot whichever is the greater.

(5) Openings in the sail, in addition to the normal cringles and reefing eyelets, are permitted provided that the sail is flat in the vicinity of the openings.

(6) When batten pockets are measured the maximum inside dimensions shall be taken, ignoring the effect of any elastic or other retaining devices. The length shall be taken from the aft edge of the sail.

(7) Sails passing round a stay or spar and attached back on themselves by stitching, zipper or similar device shall be considered to be double luffed sails.

(8) If the luff of the sail is not attached to a spar or luff wire, a check wire, minimum diameter 1·25 mm, shall be securely fastened to the head and tack cringles. The length of the luff shall be measured with sufficient tension to straighten this check wire.

(9) Where sails are set on spars, measurement bands shall be marked on the spars, so that they are clearly discernible whilst racing. The inside edges of these bands shall define the limits to which the sail may be set.

## 3. Headsails

(1) The length of the luff shall normally be the distance between the lowest part of the sail on the luff rope at the tack and the highest point of the sail on the luff rope at the head.

Owing, however, to the varying methods of making the corners of headsails, a measurer shall, if he considers that a sail is measured either favourably or unfavourably by this method, use a different method as follows:

The point of measurement at the tack shall be the point where the extension of the luff meets the extension of the foot, ignoring any round or hollow to the foot, and the point of measurement at the head shall be the point where the extension of the luff meets the extension of the leech, ignoring any round or hollow of the leech.

If the cloth is not permanently attached to a luff wire, the measurer shall be satisfied that the luff cannot be stretched to exceed the maximum dimension permitted by the rules.

(2) The length of the leech shall normally be the distance between the lowest part of the sail directly below the centre of the clew cringle and the highest part of the sail at the head.

(3) The length of the foot shall normally be the distance between the lowest point of the sail on the luff rope and the outer edge of the sail directly aft of the centre of the clew cringle.

(4) The measurement from clew to luff shall normally be between the outside edge of the clew and the nearest point on the luff.

## 5. Spinnakers

(1) The spinnaker shall be measured folded along its centreline with the leeches together.

(2) The length of the leeches shall

be taken as the distance between the highest point of the sail at the head and the lowest point of the sail on the leech, measured round the edge of the sail.

(3) The half-width of the foot shall be taken as the distance between the lowest points on the centre fold and leech, measured round the foot of the sail.

(4) The length of the centre fold shall be taken as the distance between the head and the mid-point of the foot, measured round the fold of the sail.

(5) The half-height half-width shall be taken as the distance between the points on the leech and the centre fold which are, measured in a straight line, half the maximum permitted leech length from the head.

(6) The three-quarter height half-width shall be taken as the distance between points on the leech and the centre fold which are, measured in a straight line, one quarter of the maximum permitted leech length from the head.

SECTION IV—SAIL AREA MEASUREMENT

## 1. General

(1) The intention is to establish a reliable and simple method of measuring the area of the sail plan, including spars. This method produces consistent results not dependent on variations in roping tensions or sophisticated measuring equipment.

(2) The principle of the measurement of the area of a mainsail, and of a headsail roped for a luff spar, is to use measurement bands, or measurement bands and the foot length recorded on the sail, to obtain the area of the main triangle and to add (or subtract) the area of the rounds on the luff, leech and foot.

(3) In the case of a sail set into a groove on a spar that area obscured within the groove shall not be included when calculating the area.

(4) The area of any holes in the sail shall not be deducted from the measured area.

(5) The term 'sail' shall be taken to include the headboard and tabling. It shall not include bolt or foot ropes or cringles which are wholly outside the sail.

## The international jury

The ORC regulations for the Level Rating Class Championships ('the Green Book') lays down that there shall be an international jury for the events. 'Its chairman shall be nominated by the organizing club with the agreement of the national authority. One of the members of the jury shall be a representative from the ORC and there shall be at least three other members.' Other international events may also declare that there is to be an international jury. As mentioned on page 19 this means that it is constituted under IYRU rule 77.6 and is not just 'a jury of different nationalities'. Because it overrules the right of appeal (a cardinal right in yacht racing) it must conform to the IYRU code. The terms of reference are as follows:

1. The international jury shall consist of:
   One president,
   One or two vice-presidents,
   Not less than three nor more than twelve other members, and
   One secretary without vote.

2. They shall be chosen by the organizing authority—subject to the approval of the IYRU—from amongst yachtsmen who have an intimate knowledge and experience of the racing rules.
3. For the purpose of racing rule 75, members shall not be regarded as 'interested parties' by reason of their nationality. Their appointment shall be made regardless of geographical considerations.
4. At least half the number of members including the president and the vice-presidents, shall form a quorum. At the discretion of the president to expedite the hearing of protests, the jury may be divided into two groups provided that each jury consists of not less than five persons.

   In the event of a division into two groups, either group may adjourn after finding the facts, and refer the case to a meeting of the full jury.
5. The president shall take the chair at meetings of the jury, and in his absence, the members present shall choose one of the vice-presidents, and in their absence, one of their number, to be chairman of such meetings.
6. Decisions by the jury shall be taken by a simple majority. The president and each vice-president and each member present in person shall have one vote. In the event of an equality of votes cast the chairman of the meeting shall have a second or casting vote.
7. The jury shall perform the following functions:

   (a) To make final decisions on all matters relating to entries and to the measurement of yachts.

   (b) To authorise any variations from or additions to:

   (i) the racing rules, such as numbers, recall procedures, etc., and

   (ii) the sailing instructions or other special instructions issued to the competitors.

   (c) To authorize the substitution of reserve crews and yachts.

   (d) To hear and decide all protests.

   (e) To offer advice to the organizing authority or the race committee(s) on such subjects as may have a direct bearing on the fairness of the competition.
8. The jury may appoint one or more of its members to assist the race committee(s) on board the committee boat(s).
9. All protests shall be heard as soon as practicable after the yachts concerned have finished.
10. Any member of the jury who speaks of his own observation of an incident shall give his evidence in the presence of the parties to the protest.
11. In accordance with racing rules 2(j) and 3.2(b)(xvi), there shall be no appeal from the decisions of the jury. Thus the jury should comply with racing rule 71 and give 'the facts and grounds' on which its decisions are based.
12. An adequate number of interpreters familiar with nautical terminology shall be at the disposal of the jury and to assist parties to protests and witnesses.
13. When the jury is constituted as above, the IYRU specifically authorizes the jury to act on its behalf at the regatta within these terms of reference.

# 3. Ownership formalities

## Choosing a boat

The shop windows for second-hand boats are the yachting journals and the yacht brokers. Most journals have large brokerage sections and also a classified section of boats offered for private sale. For obvious reasons the fact that a boat is advertised in a periodical must not be taken to mean that it has that journal's sanction. The economics of yachting are such that not even regularly placed company advertisements are scrutineered for false or optimistic claims. So the newcomer to the sport is well advised to seek help from someone fairly knowledgeable. Unlike buying a second hand car where there are booklets available indicating the market value of a particular make, model and year, yachting does not yet have such established guides, although regular reading of the classified columns will engender the potential buyer with a pretty good idea of what he should be paying for a given type of boat and condition.

The advantage of approaching a broker is that he may be able to find something that suits the client's requirements, even if he does not appear to have a suitable type on his own list. Most brokers operate some sort of liaison system, having access to other brokers' lists and thus saving the client a considerable amount of work. Naturally, although the brokerage fee is payable by the vendor the price of yachts acquired through a broker is usually higher than if bought privately, but normally the buyer will end up with something that suits him better than if he had compromised his requirements by pursuing just those boats which were advertised at the time.

## Details of transaction (UK)

Whilst his prime function is to bring together vendor and buyer the broker is in a position to assist with chartering arrangements, craft evaluation, checking of inventories and of course to look after the formalities of ownership transfer. He ensures that full payment is made before the purchaser can take over his new boat; he will prepare and hand over a Bill of Sale, and he will often be prepared to assist with Registration problems. As an example of the fee one can expect to pay a broker for handling a sale the Yacht Brokers, Designers and Surveyors Association (UK) recommends the following scale of charges, calculated on the agreed contract price:

Values up to £1,000—10%
Values between £1,000 and £5,000—8%
Values between £7,000 and £25,000—8% on the first £5,000 and 6% on the remainder.
Values over £25,000—6% on the total

## Buying second hand—get it surveyed

It hardly needs saying but when buying a second hand boat it is most advisable to have the craft surveyed. Even if the boat is well known to the purchaser there may be something amiss that has not yet made itself obviously apparent— working keelbolts, parting hull-deck joint, delamination and other like faults that sometimes plague even the best constructed vessels. Where buying through a finance company a survey will be necessary in any event and in these cases the finance company will usually suggest a surveyor.

A survey report is not just a certificate declaring whether the yacht has passed or failed but, according to the YBDSA codebook, '. . . an overall assessment of her condition from which her potential can be deduced'. A surveyor will methodically and thoroughly prod the timber for signs of rot, tap the glass reinforced plastic for signs of delamination, check the fastenings for rust, possibly draw the keelbolts for inspection, check the engine installation, the electrics, the spars and the rigging. In short the client will have a complete dossier on the boat's condition and, where relevant, suggested methods of remedying a deficient area.

Charges for survey work vary but the YBDSA gives a minimum scale of fees for different tonnages of boat and it is advisable to secure an estimate first.

## Buying new

When buying new the potential owner will either be buying a type with which he is acquainted, one which is recommended to him or one that is brought to his attention by advertisements in the yachting periodicals. In the case of the latter

particularly he should reserve a measure of caution and be objective about a builder's claims. In fact it is perfectly reasonable for a prospective buyer to commission a surveyor to produce a report for him on a new boat just as he might an old boat. Remember that in its new, sparkling condition a boat is unlikely to reveal deficiencies. This is particularly relevant when the boat is a new model. An older design will usually be well tested and the purchaser is well advised to seek the opinions of owners of that type. However, he must bear in mind that most yachtsmen will regard their boat almost as a child, often refusing to acknowledge any inadequacies of performance or construction it might have. A useful guide to the prospective buyer will be the certification that accompanies a product—for instance the Ship and Boatbuilders' National Federation and Lloyds' Register of Shipping provide such services which vary from mere approval of the building premises and methods to thorough inspections of individual boats. Details of Lloyds scheme for GRP boats are in Fig 6.

It is common sense for a prospective buyer to scan his market thoroughly, either by writing to or visiting all the firms that are able to offer him what he requires or by doing some homework at a boat show. The effort will be amply rewarded as he will be able to see what lies behind the glossy images portrayed in the advertisements.

## Registration in Britain

Registering a yacht as a British ship (which falls under HM Customs and Excise and must not be confused with registration in Lloyds' Register of Yachts)

27

## ownership

### Lloyd's Register of Shipping
Building Certificate

Up to 20 metres

LRBC

As an alternative to classification, the Society will provide a Lloyd's Register Building Certificate to newly constructed yachts which have been built of any approved material in accordance with the Society's Yacht Rules, under the supervision of the Society's Surveyors, without the requirement of mandatory periodical surveys thereafter.

This certificate will cover the standard GRP production yacht and will be issued on satisfactory completion of all stages of construction and installation of machinery and electrical equipment as shown hereafter.

(a) HMRN (Hull Moulding Release Note) A Release Note showing basic items of construction from moulded hull to the completed yacht will be issued to the Moulder/Builder to cover items inspected by the Society's Surveyors. This Note is not a certificate.

(b) HCC (Hull Construction Certificate) When all outstanding applicable items shown on the HMRN are examined and found satisfactory by the Society's Surveyors, a Hull Construction Certificate will be issued to the Moulder/Builder.

(c) MIC (Machinery Installation Certificate) When the machinery and electrical equipment has been installed under the supervision of the Society's Surveyors, a Machinery Installation Certificate will be issued to the Moulder/Builder.

(d) LRBC (Loyd's Register Building Certificate) Please note, therefore, the various stages of construction of a GRP yacht considered by the Society.

(a) = HMRN
(a) + (b) = HMRN + HCC
(a) + (b) + (c) = HMRN + HCC + MIC
(a) + (b) + (c) = LRBC

On receipt of the Hull Construction and Machinery Installation Certificates from the Moulder/Builder, an owner may apply to the Yacht and Small Craft Department for an LRBC Certificate and this will be issued. At the same time particulars of the yacht will be taken for entry in the next edition of the Society's Register of Yachts.

*Fig 6. Lloyd's scheme for GRP boats.*

28

is necessary for the acquisition of a marine mortgage. However, it is also of value from other angles:

It gives protection under the British flag when sailing in foreign waters.

It greatly simplifies the buying and selling of a yacht.

It is an internationally recognized proof of ownership.

When buying a new vessel the boat-builder will often arrange for registration on behalf of the owner. However, the following points outline the procedure of registration should the owner be conducting this himself:

Decide on the name (which must not duplicate that of any other registered ship) and submit it for approval to the Registrar General of Shipping and Seamen, Department of Trade, Llantrisant Road, Cardiff CF5 2YS. This submission will be on an official form which is available from the Registrar General or from the Registrar of British Ships at the intended port of registry. (There are over a hundred of these in the British Isles.)

Choose the port of registry—normally the one nearest your home port—and obtain from the Registrar there a Registration form.

If it is a new vessel the Registrar will require documents which establish your ownership. These will be a receipt from the builder or a building certificate. If the vessel is not new, but was previously unregistered, you will be required to submit a Builder's Certificate supplied to the original owner and a Bill of Sale for each subsequent transfer of ownership (official forms of Bill of Sale can be obtained from the Registrar of British Ships, code number 10 XS 79).

Whether the yacht is newly built or not you will be required to complete a Declaration of Ownership as evidence of your qualification as a British subject to own a British ship. This Declaration form is also available from the Registrar. When buying an already registered vessel it is advisable to ascertain whether the vendor has registered his ownership. This can be done by visiting the office of the Registrar where on payment of a small fee you can inspect the Register Book or, for a slightly greater fee, you can write for a copy of the particulars of registry from the Registrar. In each case you will be able to ascertain whether there is any mortgage outstanding.

The process of registration involves having the vessel measured for tonnage, a somewhat long-winded procedure, which was recently simplified for craft under 45 ft. in length. Application for measurement of tonnage should be made on form SUR6A (available from the Registrar or from the Royal Yachting Association). For registration of a boat that is lying in British waters the measurement application form should be submitted to the RYA or the YBDSA, and for registry of a boat lying in foreign waters it should be submitted to the YBDSA or to Lloyds' Register of Shipping. For small craft purposes the YBDSA is probably better geared to the job and with 170 members throughout the British Isles and in nine other countries, it is possibly advisable to approach that body.

Fees payable for tonnage measurement currently stand at a maximum of £35 for measurement of a boat within the UK and £70 for a pleasure craft measured abroad. However, where a yacht lying overseas is rather inaccessible to a particular measurer, additional charges may be made. For precise details about charges the RYA should be consulted.

Any alterations to a registered boat which changes its physical dimensions or modifies the internal space, such as the installation of a bigger engine, may require re-measurement.

For yachts of 45 ft and over the Registrar will issue a Carving and Marking note, bearing the official number and registered tonnage which have to be carved on the yacht's main beam. The Carving Note must be certified by a Department of Trade surveyor (or sometimes by a specially authorized HM Customs officer). When the certified note is returned to the Registrar he will register the yacht and issue a Certificate of Registry.

Similarly, the owner of a yacht under 45 ft overall will be issued with a Carving and Marking Note which explains how the yacht is to be marked. When this has been done the Carving Note is returned to the Registrar without requiring certification.

For all sizes of pleasure craft the Carving and Marking note will give directions as to how the yacht is to be marked with respect to port of registry. Membership of certain yacht clubs can alleviate the necessity of painting on the name of the port of registry, so the name of the owner's yacht club should be supplied with the first registration application. It will be apparent to the reader that the procedure of registration is quite tedious, so adequate time should be allowed for the procedure—about two months is suggested.

If any change is made to the registered particulars, such as a change of address or irredeemable damage to the yacht causing her to be written off, the Registrar should be notified. If there is a change of ownership the vendor should transfer it to the new owner by Bill of Sale (form XS79, from the Registrar) and give him the Certificate of Registry.

## Identification

The owner of an unregistered yacht is well advised to consider the problem of identification since he may be called to present his ship's papers if caught in a predicament in foreign waters. A note from the owner's yacht club may suffice, but it is as well to obtain an RYA International Certificate for Pleasure Navigation which is recognized by many European nations.

## Insurance

Boat insurance can generally be divided into four sections which will be covered by most policies.

1. Loss of the vessel or damage caused by such misadventures as sinking, collision, fire, stranding and theft. For this the maximum amount covered is the insured value of the vessel.
2. Damage caused by the Policy-holder to other vessels, piers, etc. through collision where the owner is at fault.
3. Any legal liability for injury or loss sustained by persons aboard the insured's vessel, with the exclusion of paid crew who should be insured separately under an Employer's Liability Policy.
4. Salvage charges claimed by salvors.

When taking out an insurance policy it must be remembered that any incorrect, inadequate or false information given on the proposal form might encourage the insurance company to seek to deny any liability under the policy. Due care must therefore be taken to complete the form accurately with all the information required.

The insurance company will want to know the value of the vessel. This should be near the average market value of that type and of that age. There is no point overinsuring as the compensation paid against the vessel's total loss would be no more than this market value. On the other hand, of course, the owner must not under-insure his yacht as the insurance company's liability would be the insured value and would thus be below replacement cost.

In inflationary times it is wise to adjust the insured value every year to keep abreast of the market so that the insured value is not allowed to fall below the market value. Another point to consider is that the market value of a boat insofar as the insurance company is concerned is that of the specific vessel insured rather than a new model of the same design. Consequently the total loss of a five-year old boat would not ensure that the owner was sufficiently compensated to go out and buy a brand new sistership without stumping up a little himself.

On top of the insured value the owner will obviously need to secure a third party liability cover. Most insurance companies of course provide this facility, but it is imperative to make sure that the amount of coverage is adequate, and that doesn't mean thousands but tens of thousands. An indemnity of about £50,000 would be about the minimum.

Most marine insurers offer different terms for different types of sailing, or more specifically for different territorial limits. The owner should think carefully about the nature of his sailing, but if he decides to economize on the premium by restricting himself to coastal sailing, for instance, he must be sure to inform his insurance company before embarking on an extended cruise as he may find he is not covered. It is usually possible to negotiate with an insurance company for temporary modifications to the policy, but it is of course imperative that the Policy-holder should give his insurers due notice.

The three territorial limits which are usually defined by different scales of charges are, in ascending cost:
1. Non-tidal waters of the United Kingdom.
2. Coastal cruising within ten miles of the yacht's permanent mooring place.
3. Full coastal and seagoing cruising within the home trade limits, which cover all United Kingdom waters and continental coasts from Brest to Elbe.

For cruising farther afield a different cover will be required.

Another type of option open to the yacht owner is the length of the in-commission period. Whereas the yacht will be covered for the full twelve months it will naturally be cheaper for him if he can establish in advance the duration which his boat will be used. If she is going to be laid up for eight months of the year, it will save the owner on his premium if he declares this rather than be forced to pay for twelve months in commission. Stretching the period may not necessarily imply increased premium but the insurers must be notified otherwise they may subsequently reject a claim.

When paying for insurance the cover

commences from the day of payment and not necessarily from the day the receipt arrives. In the case of urgency the date of payment may be certified at a Post Office or Bank. (As in the case of motor insurance most marine insurers offer a voluntary excess clause which may reduce the premium.)

When marine insurance expires, it expires. There are no such things as days of grace and although most insurance companies will send reminders, they are not legally obliged to do so. So the Policy-holder is well advised to make careful note of the relevant date.

Insurance cover for personal belongings should be treated as a separate category from normal marine insurance. Although a marine insurance does to some extent cover personal loss it is subject to a maximum of £500 and £50 per item.

Insurance for trailing a boat is rather a complicated matter. Broadly speaking when a boat is being trailed it will be covered by the owner's motor insurance policy, but when the trailer is unhitched to commence marine operations the cover will revert to the boat's insurance policy. The full extent of coverage for trailing may vary from one insurance company to another so their advice should be sought before commencing haulage operations.

A separate cover is given to racing as opposed to cruising and in most cases claims with respect to such things as sails, spars and rigging will be covered but only to the tune of two-thirds the replacement cost.

When race damage is the result of a collision most insurance companies will take the result of the protest hearing to establish liability and some will reject a claim if an incident was not taken as far as the protest room.

Coverage against theft is a normal part of any insurance policy, be it theft of the entire vessel or just some of its equipment. However, theft will only be covered if it was preceded by forcible entry so the yacht owner will have to satisfy his insurance company that a stolen item was properly locked away and not presented as an open invitation to the thief. Outboard motors, for instance, should be fitted with an anti-theft lock.

Similarly, the insurance company will expect the owner to act in a reasonable fashion when it comes to looking after his yacht. It would not go down well if the owner were to lay his mooring just off a potentially hazardous exposed shore and any resulting claim could well be prejudiced against. In fact some areas carry increased premiums by virtue of their exposed nature.

### Legalities of ownership
*Importing a yacht on a temporary basis* (Ref. HM Customs and Excise Notice No. 8A Nov. 75)

Importing a yacht into the United Kingdom is subject to the payment of import duty and Value Added Tax. However, a privately-owned vessel *temporarily imported* by a person resident outside the UK and used '. . . solely for his own or dependants' personal use may be admitted without payment of duty and VAT . . .' for a period prescribed by set circumstances.

Notice No. 8A: 'For the purpose of this relief a person is regarded as *resident outside the United Kingdom*:
(a) if during the period of 24 months ending on the date of his arrival into the

United Kingdom he has been outside the United Kingdom for a period of, or for periods together amounting to, not less than 12 months; or

(b) if he has left the United Kingdom to take up residence abroad for a period intended to exceed 12 months, and returned temporarily to the United Kingdom within a period of 12 months from the date of his departure.

For importers who qualify under sub-paragraph (a) above the maximum period of relief is 12 months; for those who qualify under sub-paragraph (b) 6 months. The Commissioners of Customs and Excise have power to reduce periods in individual cases; in particular, if a person has recently benefited for more than 6 months duty and VAT free use of a private vessel, the period of relief may be limited to one month.

There are provisos attached to this though, one particularly significant one being that '. . . the vessel must not be, or be offered, exposed or advertised to be sold, lent, pledged, hired, given away, exchanged or otherwise disposed of in the United Kingdom. It may be employed only for the personal use of the importer, or while he remains in the United Kingdom, of his dependants'.

If a foreign boat present in UK waters is offered for sale in the UK any import duty and VAT payable *will be payable on the gesture of intent to sell* and not on the eventuality of the boat actually being sold. Not very long ago an American Admiral's Cup yacht lying in the UK was placed in the hands of a yacht broker and an advertisement taken in a yachting periodical. The owner evidently wasn't aware that his yacht would be liable to duty unless actually sold and on his refusal to remit the duty payable his boat

was impounded until the matter was finally cleared. Technically, any infringement of this importation law, however trivial it may seem, could force the owner to forfeit his vessel.

Note also that the law states the vessel must be used only for the importer's personal use or that of his dependants. The expression *dependant* is taken to mean '. . . husband or wife of that person (the importer) or any other person wholly or mainly maintained by him or in his custody, charge or care'.

When an owner does bring a foreign yacht into the UK he has to claim for relief from duty and taxation on form C782 which is supplied by the Customs Officer. Despite the permitted maximum periods of stay given in a previous paragraph a vessel must depart British waters when the owner does so, or on the date recorded on C782 if this is earlier. Again, failure to comply with this may result in the forfeiture of the vessel although if it is impracticable to move the boat out at the same time the Customs Office should be notified.

When the Customs officer is satisfied that the importer is eligible for temporary importation relief the officer will return the first two pages of form C782 to the importer who must then retain them on board and be prepared to present them if required at any time during the vessel's stay.

If spare parts and accessories are required for a vessel on temporary importation relief these may also be brought in duty and tax free provided the local Customs man is notified first and the import properly arranged. Where a boatyard or other person acts as an agent in bringing in these parts the first two pages of C782 should be presented to that third party.

Where an owner intends to stay in the UK for twelve months or more, he may import a vessel free of VAT and duty if he has owned it and used it abroad for at least twelve months (not necessarily in one continuous period) before his arrival. However, it is a further condition that the boat should not '. . . be offered, exposed or advertised to be lent, hired, pledged, given away, exchanged, sold or otherwise disposed of in the United Kingdom within a period of two years of either the date of importation or the date of the importer's arrival in the United Kingdom for a stay of at least 12 months, whichever is the later'. Naturally enough, the Customs Officer will want to see evidence that that boat was used by the owner in the previous twelve months and to this end the owner should submit receipted purchase invoice, foreign registration papers and insurance documents.

Where a yacht arrives into the country in advance of its owner, it cannot be released under the temporary importation relief until the owner arrives. However, it may, under certain conditions, be released '. . . for storage unused under security of a bond or a deposit equal to the Customs charges potentially due while awaiting his arrival'. The owner's application for relief from Customs charges will then, and only then, be considered when he arrives.

### Exporting a vessel under its own power

Particulars of vessels purchased in the United Kingdom for direct export under their own power should be entered on HM Customs and Excise form C273 which should be endorsed 'Export of boat other than as cargo'. This form should be completed in duplicate and both copies sent to the Customs office together with a notification of the intended departure date, the name, nationality and tonnage of the vessel, and the name and address of the owner. Where the vessel is to be zero-rated for the purpose of VAT the duplicate copy should be endorsed in red 'For VAT purposes only'.

### Going Foreign

References

Very comprehensive information on the legal and practical aspects of going foreign is provided in three booklets published by the Royal Yachting Association entitled *Planning for Going Foreign*. Volume I contains general information about voyaging overseas and specific information about Belgium, Denmark, France (North and West), Holland, Ireland, United Kingdom and West Germany; Volume II covers Finland, Norway and Sweden and Volume III deals with Mediterranean France, Greece, Italy, Malta, Portugal, Spain, Turkey and Yugoslavia. It is recommended that any yachtsman proposing to undertake a voyage that will take him out of home waters should study these booklers as they contain a considerable amount of information that cannot be condensed into the space available here. Other extremely useful sources of information are the Cruising Association Handbook and Reed's Nautical Almanac.

### Checklist for Going Foreign

*Documentation:* Before embarking on a foreign voyage the skipper of the yacht should notify the local HM Customs and Excise branch, filling in the relevant form which will be provided by the office.

The sort of information required is the destination, date of departure, number of persons aboard, their nationalities, estimated date and place of arrival back in the United Kingdom. Upon return the yacht and crew will have to be cleared by Customs or Public Health Officer and naturally there will be another form to be filled then.

*Ship's papers:* Registration papers, if the yacht is registered. If she is unregistered, an International Certificate for Pleasure Navigation (from the RYA or equivalent national authority), a covering note from the owner's yacht club or cruising authority, and a bill of sale, charter agreement or any other document which gives adequate details of the vessel, will usually suffice.

*Duty and tax:* Naturally most things purchased overseas will be subject to import duty and Value Added Tax. However, most countries give an allowance on certain commodities and quantities which is duty-free. At the time of writing the duty-free allowances in the UK are as below.

*Bonded Stores:* Yachts voyaging beyond Brest to the south and the North Bank of the Elbe to the north may ship duty-free stores. This concession requires formal outward clearance by HM Customs and Excise and the stores, which will be placed on board in a sealed locker, must not be opened until the imaginary boundaries are passed.

*Passports* for all crew members.

| | If you have come from an EEC country **and** the goods were **not** bought in a duty-free shop or on a ship or aircraft | If you have come from a country outside the EEC **or** if the goods were bought in a duty-free shop or on a ship or aircraft |
|---|---|---|
| **TOBACCO GOODS** | | |
| Cigarettes | 300 | 200 |
| **or** Cigarillos | 150 | 100 |
| **or** Cigars | 75 | 50 |
| **or** Tobacco | 400 grammes | 250 grammes |
| **ALCOHOLIC DRINKS** | | |
| over 38·8° proof (22° Gay-Lussac) | 1½ litres | 1 litre |
| **or** not over 38·8° proof | 3 litres | 2 litres |
| **or** Fortified or sparkling wine | 3 litres | 2 litres |
| **and** Still table wine | 3 litres | 2 litres |
| The allowances above are not for persons under 17 | | |
| **PERFUME** | 75 grammes (3 fl oz) | 50 grammes (2 fl oz) |
| **TOILET WATER** | ⅜ litres | ¼ litres |
| **OTHER GOODS** | £50 worth | £10 worth |

# ownership

*Flags and Signals:* Ensign, courtesy flags for the countries intended to be visited and International Code Flag Q (yellow). Red and white lights should be rigged for night arrival (with the red light about 2 metres above the white light), but in practice this is not always complied with on small boats.

*Taking a chartered or borrowed vessel abroad:* The owner or charterer should apply in writing for a licence from the Collector of Customs and Excise at the yacht's home port or starting port for the cruise. The application should contain particulars of the vessel, names and addresses of the owner and the person under whose charge the vessel will be during the intended voyage, the period and purpose for which the licence is required. The licence should be carried on board together with the Charter Party (which shows that the crew has the owner's permission to use his vessel).

## Importing a yacht into the US

A yacht imported into the United States for sale or charter to a US resident is liable for import duty whether it arrives as cargo or under its own power. (The only exception, seldom applicable today, pertains to yachts contracted for sale or charter before December 1, 1927.) Any boat imported into the US must prominently display a label certifying that it conforms to the current Coast Guard regulations and safety standards. For information about how to obtain a label of certification, contact the Commander of the nearest US Coast Guard District.

## Bringing a yacht into the US on a temporary basis

Cruising Licences

After making formal entry into a port of arrival in the United States, the owner of a foreign-owned yacht can apply for a license to cruise in US waters for a period up to six months without obtaining formal clearances, paying entry fees, tonnage taxes, and so forth. But a cruising license will be issued only if the foreign yacht meets the following requirements:

1. The boat must be 'documented'— that is, it must have documented proof that it is a vessel of a particular country. Any official written proof of a yacht's country of origin, such as a letter from the home consulate or the vessel's register, will be accepted by US Customs as valid documentation.

2. The boat must come from a country that allows US yachts to sail in its waters without obtaining clearance or paying dues, taxes, or other charges. The following countries currently extend these privileges to US-owned boats: Argentina, Australia, Bahama

Islands, Bermuda, Canada, Federal Republic of Germany, Great Britain (including Turks and Caicos Islands, St. Vincent, and the territorial waters of the Northern Grenadine Islands, the Cayman Islands, the St. Christopher-Nevis-Anguilla Islands, and the British Virgin Islands), Greece, Honduras, Jamaica, Liberia, Netherlands, and New Zealand. You can check with the nearest US Customs office to find out the latest changes in this list.

When a cruising license is issued it is done under the assumption that the foreign-owned boat will comply with all US laws, that it will not engage in trade, and that it will not be chartered.

The first step is to obtain from the Customs Service the form 'Application for a cruising license—Treasury Department, US Customs Service': this simply describes the yacht, her intended cruising ground and particulars of owner. If this is accepted the department issues 'License to cruise in the waters of the United States'.

### Reporting arrival

Although a foreign yacht possesses a valid cruising license, its owner must still report his arrival in any US port he enters, even when he is coming from another US port. The report of arrival must be made to the US Customs Service within 24 hours after docking. Failure to report arrival is technically punishable by confiscation of the vessel, a fine of up to $1000, and additional fines of $500 for each person who leaves the boat and $500 for each piece of baggage that is taken ashore.

### Entry procedures for undocumented, foreign-owned yachts

Yachts that are foreign-owned and are not considered properly documented by US Customs are not eligible for cruising licenses. Such boats are required to follow certain procedures and make certain payments upon entering any US port. These are:

1. Report of arrival (required within 24 hours)
2. Formal entry and clearance (required within 48 hours)
3. Entry and clearance fees ($1·50 for entry and $1·50 for clearance for vessels under 100 net tons; $2·50 for each function for vessels 100 net tons or more)

(It is also worth noting that when the owner of a vessel requests the services of a Customs official before 8.00 a.m. or after 6.00 p.m. on work days, or any time on Sundays or holidays, he must pay the official an overtime fee of $25.)

### Imported articles

Nonresidents of the United States arriving on private, foreign-owned boats can bring the following articles into the country duty-free:

1. Clothing, jewelry, and other personal effects owned by the person at the time of his departure for the US and intended for his own use.
2. Not over 50 cigars, or 300 cigarettes, or 3 pounds of tobacco, and not over one quart of alcoholic beverages intended for personal consumption.
3. Not more than $100 worth of merchandise intended for gifts (including no more than one gallon of alcoholic beverages and 100 cigars), as long as the person has not claimed this tariff exemption within the last

six months and as long as he intends to stay in the US for at least 72 hours.

## Pollution control regulations

It is estimated that 48 million Americans went boating in 1974, and every day each one accumulated an average of one pound of paper trash, cans, and bottles plus one half pound of food wastes. This means that almost 1 million tons of garbage are thrown into the sea in one season's sailing off the coast of the USA. American law prohibits depositing refuse of any kind into coastal waters. The Coast Guard requests that all sailors put their garbage in plastic bags which can be sealed and stored in the lazarette until they can be disposed of ashore.

The discharge of oil and other liquid pollutants into US waters is also prohibited by law, and a US yacht must carry a plaque next to its engine bay which states this. Anyone who discharges enough oil or oily waste into the water to cause a film or sheen on the surface is subject to a fine of $5000. Accidental discharges must be reported to the Coast Guard immediately. And all persons who see oil being discharged from any kind of boat, pleasure or commercial, are urged to report it by calling a special toll-free number (800-424-8802).

Other pollution control regulations apply to the discharge of raw sewage. All boats with toilet facilities, the construction of which was started on or after January 30, 1975, must be equipped with one of three types of marine sanitation devices (MSD's). Type I is equivalent to a macerator-chlorinator and is designed to discharge treated waste. Type II is similar to a chloride secondary plant and discharges more thoroughly treated waste than type I. And type III is a holding tank,

recirculator, or incinerator model which is designed to discharge no waste. Eventually, however, the US pollution abatement plan calls for a no discharge system for all boats, including foreign vessels, using US waters.

## Taking a yacht from the US abroad

US residents taking a boat abroad should report their activities to the nearest Customs office and obtain clearance for departure. They should also provide information as to their destination, their estimated date of return, and a list of the names and nationalities of all crew members aboard. It is also a good idea to check with your insurance company, since many policies cover sailing in coastal waters only.

## COAST GUARD DISTRICTS AND ADDRESSES OF DISTRICT COMMANDERS

| NO. | ADDRESS | WATERS OF JURISDICTION |
|---|---|---|
| FIRST . . . . . . . . . | J. F. Kennedy Federal Building. 150 Causeway Street, Boston, Mass. 02114 PHONE: 617-223-3634 | Maine, New Hampshire, Massachusetts, and Rhode Island to Watch Hill. |
| SECOND . . . . . . . | Federal Bldg., 1520 Market Street, St. Louis, Mo. 63103 PHONE: 314-622-4605 | Mississippi River System, except that portion of the Mississippi River south of Baton Rouge, Louisiana, and the Illinois River north of Joliet, Illinois. |
| THIRD . . . . . . . . . | Governors Island, New York, N.Y. 10004 PHONE: Day–212-264-8739 PHONE: Night–212-264-4800 | Rhode Island from Watch Hill, Connecticut, New York, New Jersey Pennsylvania, and Delaware, not including the Chesapeake and Delaware Canal. |
| FIFTH . . . . . . . . . | Federal Building, 431 Crawford Street, Portsmouth, Virginia, 23705 PHONE: 804-393-9611 | Maryland, Virginia, North Carolina, District of Columbia, and the Chesapeake and Delaware Canal. |
| SEVENTH . . . . . . | 51 Southwest First Avenue, Miami, Fla. 33130 PHONE: 305-350-5621 | South Carolina, Georgia, Florida to 83° 50' W, and Puerto Rico and adjacent islands of the United States. |
| | Commander, Greater Antilles Section, U.S. Coast Guard, San Juan, Puerto Rico. PHONE: 722-2174. | Immediate jurisdiction of waters of Puerto Rico and adjacent islands of the United States. |
| EIGHTH . . . . . . . . | Room 328, Customhouse, New Orleans, La. 70130. PHONE: 504-527-6234 | Florida from 83° 50' W., thence westward, Alabama, Mississippi, Louisiana, and Texas. |
| NINTH . . . . . . . . . | New Federal Office Building, 1240 East 9th Street, Cleveland, Ohio 41199 PHONE: Day – 216-522-3950 PHONE: Night – 216-522-3983 | Great Lakes and St. Lawrence River above St. Regis River. |
| ELEVENTH . . . . . | Heartwell Building, 19 Pine Avenue, Long Beach, Calif. 90802 PHONE: 213-590-2311 | California, south of latitude 34° 58' N. |

## ownership

| | | |
|---|---|---|
| TWELFTH . . . . . . | Appraisers Building, 630 Sansome St., San Francisco, Calif. 94126. PHONE: 415-556-2560 | California, north of latitude 34° 58′ N. |
| THIRTEENTH . . . | Alaska Building, 618 Second Avenue, Seattle, Wash. 98104 PHONE: 206-624-2902 | Oregon, Washington, and Idaho. |
| FOURTEENTH . . . | 677 Ala Moana Blvd. Honolulu, Hawaii 96813 PHONE: 808-546-7130 | Hawaii and the Pacific Islands belonging to the United States west of longitude 140°W. and south of latitude 42°N. |
| SEVENTEENTH . . | P.O. Box 3-5000, Federal Building, Juneau, Alaska. 99801. PHONE: 907-586-2680 | Alaska. |

# common lights under international regulations

A.

B.
C.

D.

A. Power driven vessel over 164 ft (50 metres) (Rule 23).
B. Air cushion vehicle (hovercraft) under 164 ft (50 metres).
C. Power driven vessel under 23 ft (7 metres and at less than 7 knots and (top) a vessel under oars.

D. Sailing vessel over 64 ft showing separate side lights and optional red and green all round at masthead. Sailing boat under 23 ft can show all round white light, if it is not practicable to show proper navigation lights.

41

# common lights under international regulations

E.

E. (Top) Yachts under 37 ft 4 in (12 metres) with masthead tricolour or pulpit bi-colour and separate stern light. (Bottom) Yachts 37 ft 4 in to 64 ft with all round masthead red and green or pulpit bi-colour and separate stern light. (Stern lights just show as sectors with side lights meet.)

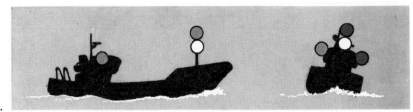

**F.**

**G.**

**H.**

**I.**

*F. Trawler (under 164 ft) with trawls out (left) and vessel fishing, but not trawling (right) (Rule 26).*
*G. Vessel restricted in ability to manoeuvre, but underway. (Rule 27.)*

*H. Towing, with length of tow less than 656 ft (200 metres) (Rule 24).*
*I. Stern view of towing vessel (any length of tow).*

# common lights under international regulations

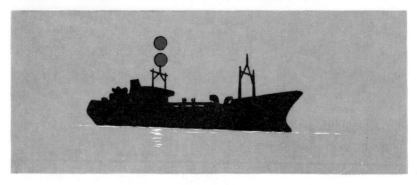

J.

K.

L.

J. Vessel not under command, not under way (Rule 27).

K. Fishing vessel under way (head on) with gear extending over 492 ft (150 metres) to port and dredger not under way and showing safe (double green) and danger (double red) sides. (Rule 27.)

L. Vessel constrained by her draft, under way. (Rule 28.)

44

# 4. International collision regulations

Revised international collision regulations are in force from July 15 1977. Care should be taken that reference is no longer made to the out-dated rules in existing books or leaflets. The new rules are known as *International regulations for preventing collisions at sea,* 1972 (IRPCS) (Since the representatives of 52 nations met in London in 1972 to formulate the rules under the auspices of IMCO, a UN agency).

The complete rules are available in UK as Cmnd 5471 (HMSO); in USA apply to the Coast Guard District Commander for the area in which it is intended to sail.

The following are of particular interest to sailing yachts.

## Part A—General

**Rule 1** *Application*
(a) These Rules shall apply to all vessels upon the high seas and in all waters connected therewith navigable by seagoing vessels.
(b) Nothing in these Rules shall interfere with the operation of special rules made by an appropriate authority for roadsteads, harbours, rivers, lakes or inland waterways connected with the high seas and navigable by seagoing vessels. Such special rules shall conform as closely as possible to these rules.

**Rule 3** *General Definitions*
(c) The term 'sailing vessel' means any vessel under sail provided that propelling machinery, if fitted, is not being used.
(d) The term 'vessel engaged in fishing' means any vessel fishing with nets, lines, trawls or other fishing apparatus which restrict manoeuvrability, but does not include a vessel fishing with trolling lines or other fishing apparatus which do not restrict manoeuvrability.
(f) The term 'vessel not under command' means a vessel which through some exceptional circumstance is unable to manoeuvre as required by these Rules and is therefore unable to keep out of the way of another vessel.
(g) The term 'vessel restricted in her ability to manoeuvre' means a vessel which from the nature of her work is restricted in her ability to manoeuvre as required by these Rules and is therefore unable to keep out of the way of another vessel.
The following vessels shall be regarded as vessels restricted in their ability to manoeuvre:
(i) a vessel engaged in laying, servicing or picking up a navigation mark, submarine cable or pipeline;
(ii) a vessel engaged in dredging,

# collision rules

surveying or underwater operations;
(iii) a vessel engaged in replenishment or transferring persons, provisions or cargo while underway;
(iv) a vessel engaged in the launching or recovery of aircraft;
(v) a vessel engaged in minesweeping operations;
(vi) a vessel engaged in a towing operation such as severely restricts the towing vessel and her tow in their ability to deviate from their course.
(h) The term 'vessel constrained by her draft' means a power-driven vessel which because of her draft in relation to the available depth of water is severely restricted in her ability to deviate from the course she is following.
(i) The word 'underway' means that a vessel is not at anchor, or made fast to the shore, or aground.

## Part B—Steering and Sailing Rules
Section 1—Conduct of Vessels in any Condition of Visibility

### Rule 5 *Look-out*
Every vessel shall at all times maintain a proper look-out by sight and hearing as well as by all available means appropriate in the prevailing circumstances and conditions so as to make a full appraisal of the situation and of the risk of collision.

### Rule 9 *Narrow Channels*
(a) A vessel proceeding along the course of a narrow channel or fairway shall keep as near to the outer limit of the channel or fairway which lies on her starboard side as is safe and practicable.
(b) A vessel of less than 20 metres in length or a sailing vessel shall not impede the passage of a vessel which can safely navigate only within a narrow channel or fairway.

Section II—Conduct of Vessels in Sight of One Another

### Rule 12 *Sailing Vessels*
(a) when two sailing vessels are approaching one another, so as to involve risk of collision, one of them shall keep out of the way of the other as follows:
(i) when each has the wind on a different side, the vessel which has the wind on the port side shall keep out of the way of the other;
(ii) when both have the wind on the same side, the vessel which is to windward shall keep out of the way of the vessel which is to leeward;
(iii) if a vessel with the wind on the port side sees a vessel to windward and cannot determine with certainty whether the other vessel has the wind on the port or on the starboard side, she shall keep out of the way of the other.
(b) For the purpose of this Rule the windward side shall be deemed to be the side opposite to that on which the mainsail is carried or, in the case of a square-rigged vessel, the side opposite to that on which the largest fore-and-aft sail is carried.

### Rule 13 *Overtaking*
(a) Notwithstanding anything contained in the Rules of this Section any vessel overtaking any other shall keep out of the way of the vessel being overtaken.
(b) A vessel shall be deemed to be overtaking when coming up with another vessel from a direction more than 22·5 degrees abaft her beam, that is, in such a position with reference to the vessel she is overtaking, that at night she would be able to see only the sternlight of that vessel but neither of her sidelights.

46

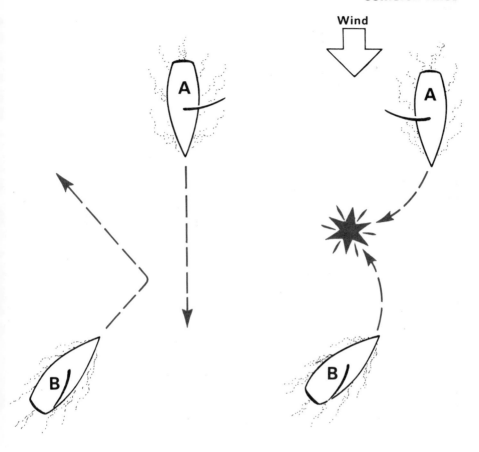

*Fig 7. Rule 12(a) (ii) Yacht B with wind on port side, and unable to determine which side sail of A is, gives way. A was on starboard gybe and so has right of way under Rule 12(a) (i) and stands on. A possible dangerous situation under IRPCS. Rule 12(a) (iii) Yacht A is on port gybe but to windward so gives way under Rule 12(a) (ii). However yacht B with wind on port side cannot determine (at night) what side yacht A has her sail (Rule 12(a) (iii)), so she also gives way. The solution is that A, realizing that she is an ambiguous case, should give way only cautiously.*

47

# collision rules

(c) When a vessel is in any doubt as to whether she is overtaking another, she shall assume that this is the case and act accordingly.

(d) Any subsequent alteration of the bearing between the two vessels shall not make the overtaking vessel a crossing vessel within the meaning of these Rules or relieve her of the duty of keeping clear of the overtaken vessel until she is finally past and clear.

**Rule 14** *Head-on Situation*

(a) When two power-driven vessels are meeting on reciprocal or nearly reciprocal courses so as to involve risk of collision each shall alter her course to starboard so that each shall pass on the port side of the other.

(b) Such a situation shall be deemed to exist when a vessel sees the other ahead or nearly ahead and by night she could see the masthead lights of the other in a line or nearly in a line and/or both side-lights and by day she observes the corresponding aspect of the other vessel.

(c) When a vessel is in any doubt as to whether such a situation exists she shall assume that it does exist and act accordingly.

**Rule 70** *Crossing Situation*

When two power-driven vessels are crossing so as to involve risk of collision, the vessel which has the other on her own starboard side shall keep out of the way and shall, if the circumstances of the case admit, avoid crossing ahead of the other vessel.

**Rule 18** *Responsibilities between Vessels*

Except where Rules 9, 10 and 13 otherwise require:

(a) A power-driven vessel underway shall keep out of the way of:
(i) a vessel not under command;
(ii) a vessel restricted in her ability to manoeuvre;
(iii) a vessel engaged in fishing;
(iv) a sailing vessel.

(b) A sailing vessel underway shall keep out of the way of:
(i) a vessel not under command;
(ii) a vessel restricted in her ability to manoeuvre;
(iii) a vessel engaged in fishing.

(c) A vessel engaged in fishing when underway shall, so far as possible, keep out of the way of:
(i) a vessel not under command;
(ii) a vessel restricted in her ability to manoeuvre.

(d) (i) Any vessel other than a vessel not under command or a vessel restricted in her ability to manoeuvre shall, if the circumstances of the case admit, avoid impeding the safe passage of a vessel constrained by her draft, exhibiting the signals in Rule 28.

(ii) A vessel constrained by her draft shall navigate with particular caution having full regard to her special condition.

(e) A seaplane on the water shall, in general keep well clear of all vessels and avoid impeding their navigation. In circumstances, however, where risk of collision exists, she shall comply with the Rules of this Part.

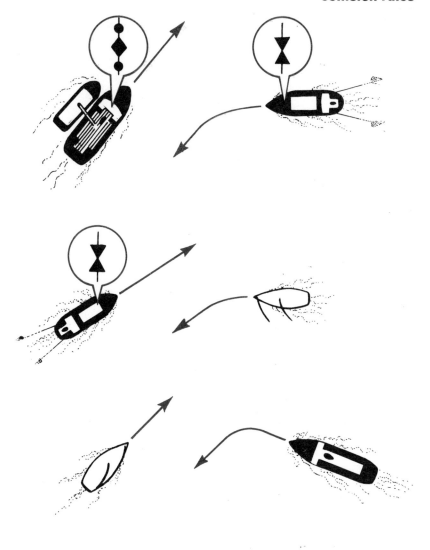

*Fig 8. Rule 18 'The right of way sequence'. Rule 18(c) A vessel 'restricted in ability to manoeuvre' has right of way over fishing boat.*

*Rule 18(d) Fishing boat has right of way over sailing vessel. Rule 18(a) Sailing vessel has right of way over power vessel.*

49

# collision rules

## Part C—Lights and Shapes

**Rule 21** *Definitions*

(a) 'Masthead light' means a white light placed over the fore and aft centreline of the vessel showing an unbroken light over an arc of the horizon of 225 degrees and so fixed as to show the light from right ahead to 22·5 degrees abaft the beam on either side of the vessel.

(b) 'Sidelights' means a green light on the starboard side and a red light on the port side each showing an unbroken light over an arc of the horizon of 112·5 degrees and so fixed as to show the light from right ahead to 22·5 degrees abaft the beam on its respective side. In a vessel of less than 20 metres in length the sidelights may be combined in one lantern carried on the fore and aft centreline of the vessel.

(c) 'Sternlight' means a white light placed as nearly as practicable at the stern showing an unbroken light over an arc of the horizon of 135 degrees and so fixed as to show the light 67·5 degrees from right aft on each side of the vessel.

(d) 'Towing light' means a yellow light having the same characteristics as the 'sternlight' defined in paragraph (c) of this Rule.

(e) 'All-round light' means a light showing an unbroken light over an arc of the horizon of 360 degrees.

(f) 'Flashing light' means a light flashing at regular intervals at a frequency of 120 flashes or more per minute.

**Rule 22** *Visibility of Lights*

The lights prescribed in these Rules shall have an intensity as specified in Section 8 of Annex I to these Regulations so as to be visible at the following minimum ranges:

(a) In vessels of 50 metres or more in length:
a masthead light, 6 miles;
a sidelight, 3 miles;
a sternlight, 3 miles;
a towing light, 3 miles;
a white, red, green or yellow all-round light, 3 miles.

(b) In vessels of 12 metres or more in length but less than 50 metres in length;
a masthead light, 5 miles; except that where the length of the vessel is less than 20 metres, 3 miles;
a sidelight, 2 miles;
a sternlight, 2 miles;
a towing light, 2 miles;
a white, red, green or yellow all-round light, 2 miles.

(c) In vessels of less than 12 metres in length:
a masthead light, 2 miles
a sidelight, 1 mile;
a sternlight, 2 miles;
a towing light, 2 miles;
a white, red, green or yellow all-round light, 2 miles.

**Rule 23** *Power-driven Vessels underway*

(a) A power-driven vessel underway shall exhibit:

(i) a masthead light forward;

(ii) a second masthead light abaft of and higher than the forward one; except that a vessel of less than 50 metres in length shall not be obliged to exhibit such light but may do so;

(iii) sidelights;

(iv) a sternlight.

(b) An air-cushion vessel when operating in the non-displacement mode shall, in addition to the lights prescribed in paragraph (a) of this Rule, exhibit an all-round flashing yellow light.

(c) A power-driven vessel of less than

7 metres in length and whose maximum speed does not exceed 7 knots may, in lieu of the lights prescribed in paragraph (a) of this Rule, exhibit an all-round white light. Such vessel shall, if practicable, also exhibit sidelights.

**Rule 25** *Sailing Vessels underway and Vessels under Oars*
(a) A sailing vessel underway shall exhibit:
  (i)  sidelights;
  (ii) a sternlight.
(b) In a sailing vessel of less than 12 metres in length the lights prescribed in paragraph (a) of this Rule may be combined in one lantern carried at or near the top of the mast where it can best be seen.
(c) A sailing vessel underway may, in addition to the lights prescribed in paragraph (a) of this Rule, exhibit at or near the top of the mast, where they can best be seen, two all-round lights in a vertical line, the upper being red and the lower green, but these lights shall not be exhibited in conjunction with the combined lantern permitted by paragraph (b) of this Rule.
(d) (i) A sailing vessel of less than 7 metres in length shall, if practicable, exhibit the lights prescribed in paragraph (a) or (b) of this Rule, but if she does not, she shall have ready at hand an electric torch or lighted lantern showing a white light which shall be exhibited in sufficient time to prevent collision.
(ii) A vessel under oars may exhibit the lights prescribed in this Rule for sailing vessels, but if she does not, she shall have ready at hand an electric torch or lighted lantern showing a white light which shall be exhibited in sufficient time to prevent collision.
(e) A vessel proceeding under sail when also being propelled by machinery shall exhibit forward where it can best be seen a conical shape, apex downwards.

**Rule 30** *Anchored Vessels and Vessels aground*
(a) A vessel at anchor shall exhibit where it can best be seen:
  (i)  in the fore part, an all-round white light or one ball;
  (ii) at or near the stern and at a lower level than the light prescribed in subparagraph (i), an all-round white light.
(b) A vessel of less than 50 metres in length may exhibit an all-round white light where it can best be seen instead of the lights prescribed in paragraph (a) of this Rule.
(c) A vessel at anchor may, and a vessel of 100 metres and more in length shall, also use the available working or equivalent lights to iluminate her decks.
(d) A vessel aground shall exhibit the lights prescribed in paragraph (a) or (b) of this Rule and in addition, where they can best be seen:
  (i)  two all-round red lights in a vertical line;
  (ii) three balls in a vertical line.
(e) A vessel of less than 7 metres in length, when at anchor or aground, not in or near a narrow channel, fairway or anchorage, or where other vessels normally navigate, shall not be required to exhibit the lights or shapes prescribed in paragraphs (a), (b) or (d) of this Rule.

## collision rules

### Part D—Sound and Light Signals

**Rule 32** *Definitions*

(b) The term 'short blast' means a blast of about one second's duration.

(c) The term 'prolonged blast' means a blast of from four to six seconds' duration.

**Rule 34** *Manoeuvring and Warning Signals*

(a) When vessels are in sight of one another, a power-driven vessel underway, when manoeuvring as authorized or required by these Rules, shall indicate that manoeuvre by the following signals on her whistle:

one short blast to mean 'I am altering my course to starboard';

two short blasts to mean 'I am altering my course to port';

three short blasts to mean 'I am operating astern propulsion'.

(b) Any vessel may supplement the whistle signals prescribed in paragraph (a) of this Rule by light signals, repeated as appropriate, whilst the manoeuvre is being carried out:

(i) these light signals shall have the following significance:

one flash to mean 'I am altering my course to starboard';

two flashes to mean 'I am altering my course to port';

three flashes to mean 'I am operating astern propulsion';

(ii) the duration of each flash shall be about one second, the interval between flashes shall be about one second, and the interval between successive signals shall be not less than ten seconds;

(iii) the light used for this signal shall, if fitted, be an all-round white light, visible at a minimum range of 5 miles, and shall comply with the provisions of Annex I.

(c) When in sight of one another in a narrow channel or fairway:

(i) a vessel intending to overtake another shall in compliance with Rule 9(e)(i) indicate her intention by the following signals on her whistle:

two prolonged blasts followed by one short blast to mean 'I intend to overtake you on your starboard side';

two prolonged blasts followed by two short blasts to mean 'I intend to overtake you on your port side';

(ii) the vessel about to be overtaken when acting in accordance with Rule 9(e)(i) shall indicate her agreement by the following signal on her whistle:

one prolonged, one short, one prolonged and one short blast, in that order.

(d) When vessels in sight of one another are approaching each other and from any cause either vessel fails to understand the intentions or actions of the other, or is in doubt whether sufficient action is being taken by the other to avoid collision, the vessel in doubt shall immediately indicate such doubt by giving at least five short and rapid blasts on the whistle. Such signal may be supplemented by a light signal of at least five short and rapid flashes.

(e) A vessel nearing a bend or an area of a channel or fairway where other vessels may be obscured by an intervening obstruction shall sound one prolonged blast. Such signal shall be answered with a prolonged blast by any approaching vessel that may be within hearing around the bend or behind the intervening obstruction.

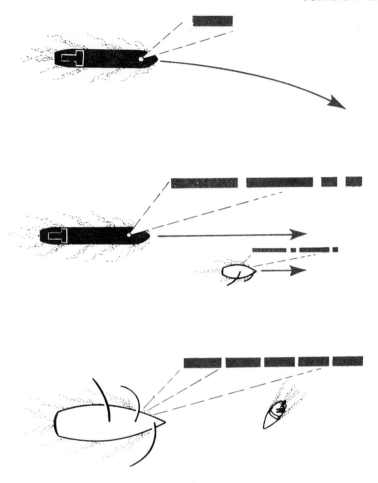

*Fig 9. Sound Signals.*
*A 'short' blast, as used when directing course to starboard, is about* one second *duration.*
*A 'prolonged' blast, as used in overtaking in rule 34(c), is 4 to 6 seconds.*
*Rule 34(d) Five 'short and rapid' blasts. In this case sounded by a boat under spinnaker and other running sails, when a fishing dinghy is seen to be in the way ahead.*

53

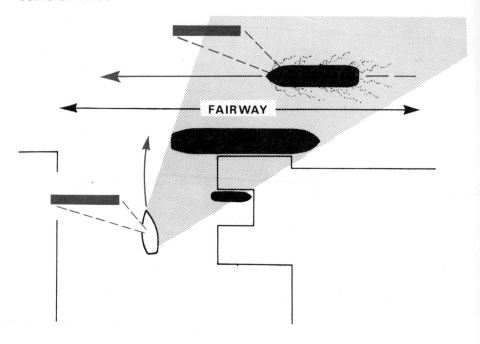

*Fig 10. Rule 34(e) One prolonged blast when unable to see round an obstruction or bend in a river: answered by a similar blast.*

(f) If whistles are fitted on a vessel at a distance apart of more than 100 metres, one whistle only shall be used for giving manoeuvring and warning signals.

**Rule 35** *Sound Signals in restricted Visibility*
In or near an area of restricted visibility, whether by day or night, the signals prescribed in this Rule shall be used as follows:
(a) A power-driven vessel making way through the water shall sound at intervals of not more than 2 minutes one prolonged blast.

(b) A power-driven vessel underway but stopped and making no way through the water shall sound at intervals of not more than 2 minutes two prolonged blasts in succession with an interval of about 2 seconds between them.
(c) A vessel not under command, a vessel restricted in her ability to manoeuvre, a vessel constrained by her draught, a sailing vessel, a vessel engaged in fishing and a vessel engaged in towing or pushing another vessel shall, instead of the signals prescribed in paragraphs (a) or (b) of this Rule, sound at intervals of not more than 2 minutes three blasts in

A

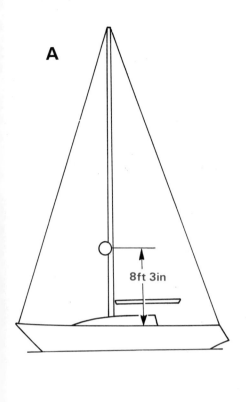

8ft 3in

B

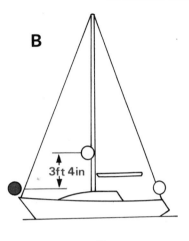

3ft 4in

c**X**

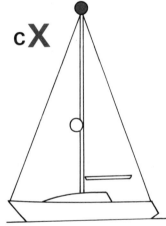

*Fig 11. Position of steaming lights for sailing boats under power (or power boats).*

*(A) For LOA exceeding 37 ft 4 in (12 metres) 'masthead' light must be 8ft 3 in (2·5 m) above 'gunwale'.*

*(B) Under 37 ft 4 in LOA masthead light may be any height but must be 3 ft 4 in (1 m) above side lights.*

*(C) This is wrong. 'Masthead' light must be above all other lights, so cannot be below tri-colour light for sailing boats.*

55

# collision rules

succession, namely one prolonged followed by two short blasts.

be shown with sidelights under it.

## Sound Signals
A vessel over '12 metres' (37 ft 3 in) is obliged to carry a whistle and bell as sound signals, in accordance with international specifications. A shorter vessel has to have 'means of making an efficient sound signal'.

## Technical requirements for lights and shapes
These are laid down in Annex I of the collision regulations. There are rules for vertical heights, spacing between lights, intensity and sectors. (Fig 11.) Note that the Offshore Rating Council Special Regulation 9.8 calls for 'Navigation Lights to be shown as required by the IRPCS mounted so that they will not be masked by sails or the heeling of the yacht'.

The RORC, however, has in addition the following more specific recommendations:

Each navigational side light bulb must have a rating of at least 10 watts, or in yachts built before 1.1.76 each sidelight may have an intensity outside the lantern of at least 1·5 candelas. Stern light bulbs must have a rating of at least 6 watts. In yachts over 40 ft LOA each side light bulb must have a manufacturer's rating of at least 25 watts.

Every yacht must carry emergency navigation lights and power source sufficient for the duration of the race. IYRU racing rule 53 states 'every yacht shall observe the IRPCS or government rules for fog signals and, as a minimum, the carrying of lights at night'.

Note: the tricolour light for yacht under 37 ft 3 in cannot be carried when under power. A 'masthead' light should

## International Distress Signals

These are laid down in Annex IV of the international collision regulations (Fig 12).

1. The following signals, used or exhibited either together or separately, indicate distress and need of assistance:

   (a) a gun or other explosive signal fired at intervals of about a minute;

   (b) a continuous sounding with any fog-signalling apparatus;

   (c) rockets or shells, throwing red stars fired one at a time at short intervals;

   (d) a signal made by radiotelegraphy or by any other signalling method consisting of the group . . . −−− . . . (SOS) in the Morse Code;

   (e) a signal sent by radiotelephony consisting of the spoken word 'Mayday';

   (f) the International Code Signal of distress indicated by N.C.;

   (g) a signal consisting of a square flag having above or below it a ball or anything resembling a ball;

   (h) flames on the vessel (as from a burning tar barrel, oil barrel, etc.);

   (i) a rocket parachute flare or a hand flare showing a red light;

   (j) a smoke signal giving off orange-coloured smoke;

   (k) slowly and repeatedly raising and lowering arms outstretched to each side;

   (l) the radiotelegraph alarm signal;

   (m) the radiotelephone alarm signal;

   (n) signals transmitted by emergency position-indicating radio beacons.

2. The use or exhibition of any of the foregoing signals except for the purpose of indicating distress and need of assistance and the use of other signals which may be confused with any of the above signals is prohibited.

Fig 12. Some international distress signals which are officially listed in IRPCS Annex IV.

N

C

MAYDAY

# 5. ORC special regulations

'Special regulations' are, as they state in their full title, for governing minimum equipment and accommodation standards. Like the rating rule they are mainly a combination of previous American and British rules and systems. They are issued in leaflet form in January each year and there are invariably annual amendments: the latest version should therefore be obtained. Space is provided below for amendments to the regulations reproduced here (as at January 1977).

In order to interpret the rules properly, several factors in their application should be understood.

1. *Purpose* The rules are to establish uniform minimum standards for the purpose of fair racing e.g. everyone has to carry a toilet as defined and cannot pursue a weight advantage by omitting it from the accommodation. The rules are not some universal formula for 'safe' racing.

2. The IYRU *racing rules* and IOR take precedence over Special Regulations (e.g. over movement or installation of equipment which could affect trim); generally there is no direct conflict. Because a yacht has an IOR rating, it does not mean that it is permitted to race. The race organizers may require an inspection to see if Special Regulations are being respected.

3. *The owner* is fully responsible for the seaworthiness of his yacht and capability of his crew. The regulations do not in any way modify this responsibility.

4. *Specifications for equipment listed.* These are not given: the equipment must be in working order and be of type, size and capacity for the use intended and size of the yacht. So it is no good carrying a sail said to be the storm jib which is not small enough and strong enough, at least in the opinion of a race official inspecting the boat. Governments, national authorities and clubs may well make specifications for yachts under their control.

5. *Local variations.* Race organizers can obviously vary the Special Regulations by cancelling, adding and amplifying. They are asked to keep such changes to a minimum, to assist the individual owner.

6. *Categories.* These are defined for races, but in practice such definitions cannot always be accurate. The organizers should select the category by checking the requirements and seeing which list is appropriate rather than searching in the definition.

## 3.0 BASIC STANDARDS

3.1 Offshore racing yachts shall be self-

60

righting, strongly built, in hull, deck and cabin top, watertight and capable of withstanding solid water and knockdowns. They must be properly rigged and ballasted, be fully sea-worthy and must meet the standards set forth herein. 'Self-righting' means that a yacht must have a positive righting arm when the mast-head, with main and foresail set, touches the water. 'Properly rigged' means (*inter alia*) that shrouds are never to be disconnected.

3.2 All equipment must function properly, be readily accessible and be of a type, size and capacity suitable and adequate for the intended use and the size of the yacht, and shall meet standards accepted in the country of registry.

4.0 INSPECTION

4.1 A yacht may be inspected at any time. If she does not comply with these special regulations her entry may be rejected, or she will be liable to disqualification or such other penalty as may be prescribed by national authority or the sponsoring organization.

5.0 CATEGORIES OF OFFSHORE EVENTS

5.1 The International Offshore Rating rule is used to rate a wide variety of types and sizes of yachts in many types of races, . . ranging from long-distance ocean races sailed in protected waters. To provide for the differences in the standards of safety and accommodation required for such varying circumstances, four categories of races are established, as follows:

5.2 *Category 1 race.* Races of long distance and well offshore, where yachts must be completely self-sufficient for extended periods of time, capable of withstanding heavy storms and prepared to meet serious emergencies without the expectation of outside assistance.

5.3 *Category 2 race.* Races of extended duration along or not far removed from shorelines or in large unprotected bays or lakes, where a high degree of self-sufficiency is required of the yachts but with the reasonable probability that outside assistance

could be called upon for aid in the event of serious emergencies.

5.4 *Category 3 race.* Races across open water, most of which is relatively protected or close to shorelines, including races for small yachts.

5.5 *Category 4 race.* Short races, close to shore in relatively warm or protected waters.

In the following lists, the star indicates the item applies to the category in that column.

6.0 STRUCTURAL FEATURES      RACE CATEGORY

|  | 1 | 2 | 3 | 4 |
|---|---|---|---|---|

6.1 *Hatches, companionways and ports* must be essentially watertight, that is, capable of being strongly and rigidly secured. Cockpit companionways, if extended below main deck level, must be capable of being clocked off to the level of the main deck at the sheer line abreast the opening. When such blocking arrangements are in place this companionway (or hatch) shall continue to give access to the interior of the hull.
   *Cockpits opening aft to the sea.* The lower edge of the companionway shall not be below main deck level as measured above. The opening   ★ ★ ★ ★ shall not be less than 50 per cent of max. cockpit depth X max. cockpit width. The requirement in 6.31 and 6.32 that cockpits must drain at all angles of heel, applies.

6.2 *Cockpits* must be struc-turally strong, self-bailing and permanently incorporated as an integral part of the hull. They must be essentially watertight, that is, all openings to the hull below the main deck level must   ★ ★ ★ ★ be capable of being strongly and rigidly secured. Any bow, lateral, central or stern well will be con-sidered as a cockpit.

# special regulations

RACE
CATEGORY
1 2 3 4

RACE
CATEGORY
1 2 3 4

6.21　The maximum volume *of all cockpits* below lowest coamings shall not exceed 6% L times B times FA. The cockpit sole must be at least 2% L above LWL.　★

6.22　The maximum volume *of all cockpits* below lowest coamings shall not exceed 9% L times B times FA. The cockpit sole must be at least 2% L above LWL.　★ ★ ★

6.33　*For yachts 21 feet rating and over.* Cockpit drains adequate to drain cockpits quickily but with a combined area (after allowance for screens, if attached) of not less than the equivalent of four ¾ in (2·0 cm) diameter drains. Yachts built before 1.1.72 must have drains with a combined area (after allowance for screens, if attached) of not less than the equivalent of two 1 in (2·5 cm) drains. Cockpits shall drain at all angles of heel.　★ ★ ★ ★

Yachts built before 1.1.77 may conform to 6.32 for races in Categories 3 and 4.

6.32　*For yachts under 21 ft rating.* Cockpit drains adequate to drain cockpits quickly but not less in combined area (after allowance for screens, if attached) than the equivalent of two 1 in (2·5 cm) diameter drains. Cockpits shall drain at all angles of heel.　★ ★ ★ ★

6.4　*Storm coverings* for all windows more than two square feet in area.　★ ★ ★

6.51　*Sea cocks or valves* on all through-hull openings below LWL, except integral deck scuppers, shaft log, speed indicators, depth finders and the like, however a means of closing such openings, when necessary to do so, shall be provided.　★ ★ ★ ★

Does not apply in Category 4 races to yachts built before 1.1.76.

6.52　Softwood plugs, tapered and of various sizes.　★ ★ ★ ★

6.6　*Life lines and pulpits:*

6.61　*For Yachts 21 ft rating and over*

6.61.1　*Taut double life-lines,* with upper life-line of wire at a height of not less than 2 ft (60 cm) above the working deck, to be permanently supported at intervals of not more than 7 ft (2·15 m).　★ ★ ★

6.61.2　*Life-line terminals.* A taut lanyard of synthetic rope may be used to secure life-lines, provided that when in position its length does not exceed 4 in (10 cm).　★ ★ ★

6.61.3　*Stanchions* shall not be angled from the point of their attachment to the hull at more than ten degrees from vertical throughout their length.　★ ★ ★

6.61.4　*Pulpits.* Fixed bow pulpit (forward of headstay) and stern pulpit (unless life-lines are arranged as to adequately substitute for a stern pulpit). Lower life-lines need not extend through the bow pulpit. Upper rails of pulpits shall be at no less height above the working deck than upper life-lines. Upper rails in bow pulpits shall be securely closed while racing.　★ ★ ★

*Fig 13. It must be possible to block off
companionways to at least main deck
level, so that the crew can still enter and
leave the yacht. Usually they will do this
by a hatch after the 'doorway' has been
blocked by washboards.*

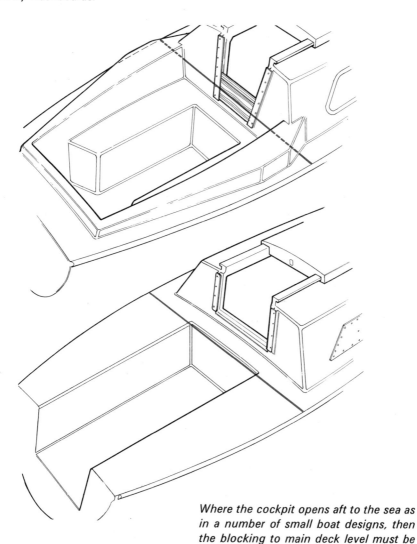

*Where the cockpit opens aft to the sea as
in a number of small boat designs, then
the blocking to main deck level must be
permanent.*

63

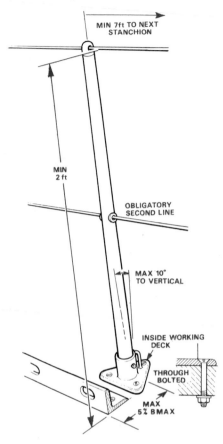

MIN 7ft TO NEXT STANCHION

MIN 2 ft

OBLIGATORY SECOND LINE

MAX 10° TO VERTICAL

INSIDE WORKING DECK

THROUGH BOLTED

MAX 5% B MAX

*Fig 14. Life-line requirements for yachts of over 21 ft rating. Note also the relationship between IOR 103.2 and special regulation 6.61.6.*

6.61.5 *Overlapping pulpits.* Life-lines need not be affixed to the bow pulpit if they terminate at, or pass through, adequately braced stanchions 2 ft (60 cm) above the working deck, set inside of and overlapping the bow pulpit, provided that the gap between the upper life-line and the bow pulpit shall not exceed 6 in (15 cm).   ★ ★ ★

6.61.6 *Pulpit and stanchion fixing.* Pulpits and stanchions shall be through-bolted or welded, and the bases thereof shall not be further inboard from the edge of the working deck than 5% of B max. of 6 in (15 cm), whichever is greater. Stanchion bases shall not be situated outboard of the working deck.   ★ ★ ★

6.62 *For Yachts under 21 ft rating*

6.62.1 *Taut single wire life-line,* at a height of not less than 18 in (45 cm) above the working deck, to be permanently supported at intervals of not more than 7 ft (2·15 m). If the life-line is at any point more than 22 in (56 cm) above the rail cap, a second intermediate life-line must be fitted. If the cockpit opens aft to the sea additional life-lines must be fitted so that no opening is greater in height than 22 in (56 cm).   ★ ★ ★

6.62.2 *Life-line terminals,* as in 6.61.2.   ★ ★ ★

6.62.3 *Stanchions,* as in 6.61.3.   ★ ★ ★

6.62.4 *Pulpits.* Fixed bow pulpit and stern pulpit (unless life-lines are arranged as to adequately substitute for a stern pulpit). Lower life-lines need not extend through the bow pulpit. Upper rails of pulpits must be at

| | RACE CATEGORY 1 2 3 4 | | RACE CATEGORY 1 2 3 4 |

no less height above the working deck than upper life-lines. Upper rails in bow pulpits shall be securely closed while racing. The bow pulpit may be fitted abaft the forestay with its bases secured at any points on deck, but a point on its supper rail must be within 16 in (40 cm) of the forestay on which the foremost headsail is hanked.   ★ ★ ★

6.62.5 *Overlapping pulpits,* as in 6.61.5, but for 2 ft read 18 in (45 cm).   ★ ★ ★

6.62.6 *Pulpit and stanchion fixing,* as in 6.61.6.   ★ ★ ★

6.63 As in 6.61 and 6.62, except that a stern pulpit is not required, provided the required height of life-line must be carried aft at least to the midpoint of the cockpit.   ★

6.7 *Ballast and Heavy Equipment.* Inside ballast in a yacht shall be securely fastened in position. All other heavy internal fittings such as batteries, stoves, gas bottles, tanks, outboard motors, etc., shall be securely fastened.   ★ ★ ★ ★

6.8 *Sheet winches* shall be mounted in such a way that operator is required to be substantially below deck.   ★ ★ ★ ★

7.0 ACCOMMODATIONS

7.11 *Toilet,* securely installed.   ★ ★

7.12 Toilet, securely installed, or fitted bucket.   ★ ★

7.2 *Bunks,* permanently installed.   ★ ★ ★ ★

7.31 *Cooking stove,* securely installed with safe accessible fuel shutoff control.   ★ ★

7.32 Cooking stove, capable of being safely operated in a seaway.   ★

7.41 *Galley facilities,* including sink.   ★ ★

7.42 Galley facilities.   ★ ★

7.51 *Water tanks,* securely installed and capable of dividing the water supply into at least two separate containers.   ★

7.52 At least one securely installed water tank, plus at least one additional container capable of holding 2 gallons.   ★

7.53 Water in suitable containers.   ★ ★

8.0 GENERAL EQUIPMENT

8.1 *Fire extinguishers,* readily accessible and of the type and number required by the country of registry, provided there be at least one in yachts fitted with an engine or stove.   ★ ★ ★ ★

8.21 *Bilge pumps,* at least two, manually operated, one of which must be operable with all cockpit seats and all hatches and companionways closed.   ★ ★

8.22 One manual bilge pump operable with all cockpit seats, hatches and companionways, closed.   ★

8.23 One manual bilge pump.   ★ ★ ★

8.31 *Anchors,* Two with cables except yachts rating under 21 ft, which shall carry at least one anchor and cable.   ★ ★ ★

8.32 One anchor and cable.   ★

8.41 *Flashlights,* one of which is suitable for signaling, water resistant, with spare batteries and bulbs.   ★ ★ ★

65

8.42   At least one flashlight, water resistant, with spare batteries and bulb. ★

8.5   *First aid kit* and manual.   ★ ★ ★ ★

8.6   *Foghorn.*   ★ ★ ★ ★

8.7   *Radar reflector.*   ★ ★ ★ ★

8.8   *Set of international code flags* and international code book.   ★

8.9   *Shutoff valves* on all fuel tanks.   ★ ★ ★ ★

### 9.0   NAVIGATION EQUIPMENT

9.1   *Compass,* marine type, properly installed and adjusted.   ★ ★ ★ ★

9.2   *Spare compass.*   ★ ★ ★

9.3   *Charts, light list and piloting equipment.*   ★ ★ ★

9.4   *Sextant, tables and accurate time piece.*   ★

9.5   *Radio direction finder.*   ★ ★

9.6   *Lead line or echo sounder.*   ★ ★ ★ ★

9.7   *Speedometer or distance measuring instrument.*   ★ ★ ★

9.8   *Navigation lights,* to be shown as required by the International Regulations for Preventing Collision at Sea, mounted so that they will not be masked by sails or the heeling of the yacht.   ★ ★ ★ ★

### 10.0   EMERGENCY EQUIPMENT

10.1   *Emergency navigation lights* and power source.   ★ ★

10.21   *Special storm sail(s)* capable of taking the yacht to windward in heavy weather.   ★ ★

10.22   Heavy weather jib and reefing equipment for mainsail.   ★ ★

10.23   *Any storm or heavy-weather jib if designed for a*   ★ ★ ★ ★

seastay or luff-groove device shall have an alternative method of attachment to the stay or a wire luff.

10.3   *Emergency steering equipment.*   ★ ★ ★

10.4   *Tools and spare parts,* including a hacksaw.   ★ ★ ★ ★

10.5   *Yacht's name* on miscellaneous buoyant equipment, such as life jackets, oars, cushions, etc. Portable sail number.   ★ ★ ★

10.61   *Marine radio transmitter and receiver* with minimum transmitter power of 25 watts. If the regular antenna depends upon the mast, an emergency antenna must be provided.   ★

10.62   *Radio receiver* capable of receiving weather bulletins.   ★ ★ ★

### 11.0   SAFETY EQUIPMENT

11.1   *Life-jackets,* one for each crew member.   ★ ★ ★ ★

11.2   *Whistles* attached to life jackets.   ★ ★ ★

11.3   *Safety belt* (harness type) one for each crew member.   ★ ★ ★

11.41   *Life raft(s)* capable of carrying the entire crew and meeting the following requirements:
   Must be carried on deck (not under a dinghy) or in a special stowage opening immediately to the deck containing life raft(s) only:)
   Must be designed and used solely for saving life at sea:
   Must have at least two separate buoyancy compartments, each of which must be automatically inflatable; each raft must be capable of carrying its rated   ★ ★ ★

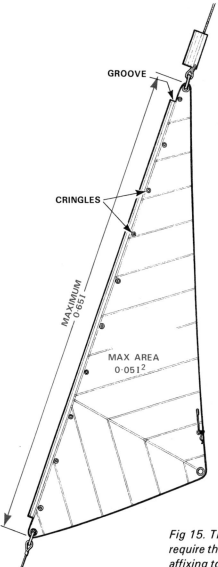

GROOVE

CRINGLES

MAXIMUM
0·65 I

MAX AREA
0·05 I$^2$

Fig 15. The storm jib. Special regulations require that this has cringles as a means of affixing to the stay other than by a groove. For all IOR classes there are maximum dimensions for the sail to qualify as a storm jib. Owners are recommended to use these same dimensions for any other offshore boat. (IOR 892)

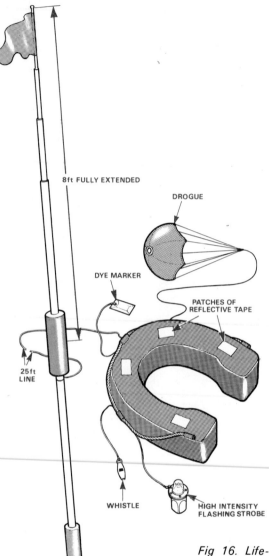

8ft FULLY EXTENDED

DROGUE

DYE MARKER

PATCHES OF
REFLECTIVE TAPE

25ft
LINE

WHISTLE

HIGH INTENSITY
FLASHING STROBE

*Fig 16. Life-rings and ancillary equip-
ment as required by special regulations.
11.53. Horseshoe life ring, high intensity
water light, drogue, dye-marker, whistle,
dan buoy with flag 8 ft off the water
and attached to ring by 25 ft of floating
line.*

68

capacity with one compartment deflated:

Must have a canopy to cover the occupants:

Must have been inspected, tested and approved within two years by the manufacturer or other competent authority; and

Must have the following equipment appropriately secured to each raft.

1 Sea anchor or drogue
1 Bellows, pump or other means for maintaining inflation of air chambers
1 Signaling light
3 Hand flares
1 Baler
1 Repair Kit
2 Paddles
1 knife

11.42   Provision for emergency      ★
water and rations to accompany raft.

11.51   *Life ring(s)*, at least one        ★
horseshoe type life ring equipped with a waterproof light and drogue within reach of the helmsman and ready for instant use.

11.52   At least one horseshoe     ★ ★ ★
type life ring equipped with a self-igniting high-intensity water light or self-igniting light having a minimum 45 minute duration and a drogue within reach of the helmsman.

11.53   At least one more horse-     ★ ★
shoe type life ring equipped with a whistle, dye marker, drogue, a self-igniting high-intensity water light, and a pole and flag. The pole is to be attached to the ring with 25 ft (8 m) of floating line and is to be of a length and so ballasted that the flag will fly at least 8 ft (2·45 m) off the water.

11.61   *Distress signals* to be     ★ ★ ★ ★

stowed in a waterproof container, and meeting the following requirements for each category, as indicated:

11.62   Twelve red parachute       ★
flares.

11.73   Four red parachute flares.    ★ ★

11.64   Four red hand flares.      ★ ★ ★ ★

11.65   Four white hand flares.     ★ ★ ★ ★

11.66   Two orange day smoke      ★ ★ ★
signals.

11.7   *Heaving line* (50 ft        ★ ★ ★ ★
(16 m) minimum length, floating type line) readily accessible to cockpit.

## New rules

Date of
amendment
Rule no. new
or existing

*January 1977*

10.22   After 'jib' add 'or heavy     ★ ★ ★ ★
weather sail in boat with no forestay.'

10.24   No mast shall have less     ★ ★ ★ ★
than two halyards.

3.3   Inboard engine installation shall meet standards accepted in the country of registry and shall be such that the engine, when running, can be securely covered, and that the exhaust and fuel supply systems are safely arranged and protected for heavy weather.

# 6. Emergency equipment stowage

The crew cannot remember where everything is stowed, nor even can the owner. This applies particularly to emergency equipment which is not normally in use. Check list is essential.

| Item | Location |
|------|----------|
| Batteries (dry) replacements | |
| Blocks, shackles (spare) | |
| Bolt croppers | |
| Bosun's chair | |
| Distress flares | |
| Dinghy repair kit | |
| Electric bulbs (replacements) | |
| (navigation and flash lights) | |
| Electronic equipment (spares) | |
| Emergency antenna | |
| Engine, spare parts | |
| Fishing line | |
| First aid Kit | |
| First aid manual | |
| Foghorn | |

Hacksaw

Halyards, spare

Harnesses

Instruction books for various fitments

Lifejackets

Long warps, tow lines

Matches, dry spare

Radar reflector

Sail number on canvas

Sail repair kit

Sail repair materials

Sail tyers

Second (mobile) bilge pump

Small fittings, split pins,

Electric fuses etc.

Soft wood plugs

Stanchions, (spares)

Starting handle, engine

Storm jib

Tools, engine

Tools, general

Winch handles (spares)

Vice, wrenches

# 7. Situations at sea

These check lists will probably be varied by every skipper, but will be servicable as aide-memoires or the basis of drills; spaces are provided for the addition of extra duties.

**Action before nightfall at sea**
Check sunset time in nautical almanac or race instructions.
Take any RDF bearing before sunset.
Check race instructions for rules (e.g. time for switching on lights, alteration of IYRU rules to international rules for prevention of collision at sea).
Ensure all crew know of change of such rules.
Check about half an hour before use is required of
   steering compass lighting
   hand bearing compass lighting
   navigation lights
   deck or sail lights
   flash lights
   chart table lighting
Check operation of mercury switch (or where checks are possible on life buoy (ring) lights).
Check white hand flares in reach of helmsmen (steamer scarers).
Is stopwatch available for timing lights?
Are crew briefed on procedure when sighting lights? (call navigator? time light themselves and note in log?).
Are any special lights expected? (e.g. oil

rigs, concentration of fishing vessels, shipping lane).
Radar reflector to be rigged or ready.
If harnesses have not been in use during day, they must now be worn at night.
LATER
Check time of dawn, then remind watch not to leave lights burning longer than necessary.

(*For owner's use*)

.................................................................

.................................................................

.................................................................

.................................................................

.................................................................

**Action in fog**
Bad visibility is insidious, so a reasonably experienced person is needed to spot when fog is becoming dangerous.

Alert navigator and skipper.
Hoist radar reflector.
Have fog signal to hand.
Sound fog signal (note new collision regulations: sailing vessel sounds 1 long 2 short blasts at interval of not more than 2 minutes).
Life-jackets available or worn (in cases of collision).

Hands on deck as required (to keep all round look out, or so as not be trapped below in event of serious collision).

Crew instructed to report lighthouse, lightship etc. fog signals to navigator, but note following:

*Fog signals are not reliable because* (a) there are areas where the signal may be inaudible, (b) Fog may not present at the light ship etc., but may be a few miles off, surrounding the yacht, (c) some fog signals may be slow in starting up for technical reasons, (d) a signal with combination high/low note or bell may only be partly audible.

Ships unfortunately now frequently disregard collision regulations and do not use audible fog signals as they should under international law.

Check engine can start immediately: run in neutral if necessary.

*Forcasting fog.* This can be done by observing both air and sea surface temperature at regular intervals together with the humidity of the air (by 'wet and dry bulb' thermometers). If sea surface temperature converges with dew point, fog will probably form. (Consult Marine Observers' Handbook NP 514—British Ministry of Defence publication.)

**Action when winds over 35 knots expected**

Crew put on heavy weather clothing and harnesses.

Close sink, lavatory sea cocks as necessary.

Check bilge pump and pump bilge dry.

Make smaller headsails and storm canvas more readily available in lockers, fo'c'sle etc.

Fix strong backs to hatches.

Hoist radar reflector (visibility will be bad and reflector will be difficult to hoist in very strong winds).

Check reef pennants rove off and reef pennant winches ready.

Halyards unlikely to be used (e.g. spinnaker) set up and secured.

Shut down ventilators as necessary.

*Navigator.* Bring dead reckoning position up to date and get any fixes before conditions deteriorate.

*Cook.* Cook meal before conditions deteriorate. Ensure 'emergency food', biscuits, chocolate, tea, etc. are easily used without having to rummage.

Check stowage of loose gear which could be dislodged on excessive heeling or knock-down.

Heavy gear which could cause injury to be restowed, if necessary.

Check anchorage of batteries, anchors and other heavy gear.

Check (if used) sea anchor, warps for streaming are available.

Check wash boards and companionway entrance.

Record barometer reading at frequent intervals (or observe barograph, if carried).

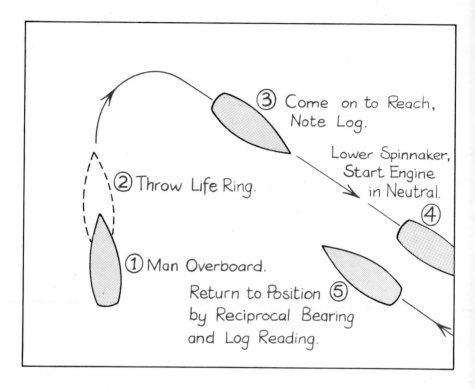

Fig 17. An example of a man overboard plan which each owner can sketch for his own particular drill. Something like this should be attached to the bulkhead, so that it is noticed at once by crew coming aboard.

## Man overboard

Before leaving harbour. Do all crew members know drills to be employed; how to release emergency equipment; the best way to haul someone out of the water on the particular boat?

*Even in light weather it is extremely difficult to see a small object in the water at a few boat lengths.*

Throw first life ring and its attached equipment.

Skipper or watch master details one man to keep visual contact with the man overboard and *do nothing else.*

Helmsman comes on to reach (which would permit reciprocal course) and notes course.

Navigator (or skipper) notes time and (if possible) log to nearest one hundredth of mile from man overboard and course change.

Start engine in neutral.

Lower spinnaker and other running sails if in use.

When gear is clear, tack or gybe on to reciprocal of reaching course.

Navigator notes time and log.

(a) Crew stand-by with second life ring (including dan-buoy) and throwing device and line. (b) Crew stand by with boarding aids (boarding ladder, looped warps, small jib as sling etc)

With yacht near man but out of reach use (a)

With man secured alongside use (b).

*At night:* bring search light (or nearest) equivalent) on deck.

*Use of engine:* depends on installation and skipper's decision.

It is again emphasized that the above is only a check list; especially for 'man overboard' procedures, each skipper will have his own views and his own drills. Equipment will also vary. Possibly a diagram (Fig 17) pasted to bulkhead will be a clear reminder for the crew.

## Action after impact damage suspected

Reduce sail (if already pressed and if position and sea room permit).

Issue life-jackets to all crew.

Raise cabin sole etc for bilge water inspection.

Check for inflow.

*If no inflow* check damage to skin fittings, speedo impellers, propeller shaft, rudder and steering.

*If there is inflow:*

Get tools, softwood plugs and repair materials clear of bilge water.

Switch on RT for transmission of MAY DAY, if necessary.

Make ready, but do not yet launch life-raft.

Part of crew then improvize repair, other part prepare for abandonment, should it prove necessary.

The US Coast Guard runs courses on boating safety which cover many of the topics mentioned above. For further information, contact the Director of the Coast Guard Auxiliary nearest you. Numbers and addresses of US Coast Guard Districts are given on page 39.

# 8. Ropes and rigging

Virtually one hundred per cent of all ropes are now synthetic—they are considerably stronger and more suitable to their tasks than the out-dated fibre ropes and they last a great deal longer. As far as strength is concerned, most modern ropes are far in excess of the minimum breaking load required; the reason is that if a synthetic rope was chosen to be of just adequate strength for a given purpose it would be too thin to handle with any comfort.

However, different types of synthetic rope vary in their suitability for given tasks and, as has always been the case, their performance and longevity will depend on the way they are treated.

Rope should not be nipped around a deadeye or shackle as the load will be taken by a few filaments only with the others put under compression.

Kinks in ropes should never be pulled out—they should be chased along to the end of the coil or else the warp should be streamed astern, whence the motion through the water will do the trick.

If it is possible to choose between a knot and a splice, the splice should be used, as long as it is a good one, since a suitable splice does not detract anything like as much from the strength of the rope as a knot.

One should regularly end-for-end sheets, guys and rope halyards so that chafe is distributed and the life of the rope doubled. With sheets and guys it is advisable to start off with over-size rope and, as the ends chafe on turning blocks, these can be trimmed off and the severed ends resealed and served.

Sheaves should be of a diameter at least three times the diameter of the rope that passes through them otherwise they will be nipping the rope.

Wash salt crystals out of rope as frequently as possible as they harden the fibre and cause internal abrasion. Sheets, in particular, should always remain supple.

The three families of plastics that more or less cover the range of synthetic ropes made are polyamide, polyester and polyolefin. *Polyamide* covers the nylons, *polyester* filament is normally known as Terylene or Dacron, whilst *polyolefins* include polypropylenes among other types. These vary in their suitability for different applications: polyamides have a high tensile strength and quite considerable elasticity; polyester filaments are almost as strong, but less susceptible to stretch and are also very *hard wearing,* and polyolefins in the form of polypropylenes are not as strong as either of the polyamides or polyesters but are light and less expensive. *Warning.* With excellent modern finishes, the ropes are often not readily distinguishable at first glance.

## The right rope for the job

APPLICATION   RECOMMENDED TYPE

Anchor warps   *Polyamide (Nylon)*
Strong but elastic — with excellent shock absorbent property. Plaited nylon most suitable as it will lay better when un-coiled. About 4 metres of chain should be incorporated between the nylon which itself should be four or five times greatest depth of water anticipated and the anchor to help the anchor take on the seabed. Polyester three strand is however stronger and less susceptible to chafe.

Halyards   *Polyester (Terylene/Dacron)*
For rope halyards use pre-stretched varieties, but watch for chafe points. (Pre-stretched is liable to kink.) For halyards where a rope tail on wire is preferred use braided polyester as it is kinder on the hands and will lie better when bundled.

Sheets   *Polyester (Terylene/Dacron)*
Braided polyester should be used as it is kind to the hands and has a good frictional surface for gripping the winch drum. It will also lie well on the sole of the cockpit.

Control lines   *Polyester (Terylene/ Dacron) or Polyolefin (Polypropylene)*
Braided polyester for heavier work, possibly polypropylene for lighter applications. Different colours available nowadays which facilitate easier identification.

Mooring warps   *Polyamide (Nylon) or Polyolefins (Polypropylene)*
Nylon is strong and shock-absorbent but the cheaper polypropylene is usually adequate if renewed periodically.

In dealing with the miles of rope that can accumulate on the cockpit sole the best solution is to have canvas bags mounted on the cockpit sides into which the rope can be bundled. It is essential for the subsequent free running of the rope that it is fed in systematically, starting with the tail end. Alternatively the rope may be coiled and hung on its own cleat by taking a loop through the coil and on to the horn of the cleat, but no complicated knots should be used as it may have to be uncoiled by another crewman, and possibly in the dark and wet.

Synthetic ropes will very soon in their life develop a surface hairiness, but this is not an indication of chafe and the rope may — as long as it is properly looked after — remain serviceable for a number of years.

## Colour codes
Most of the rope manufacturers now produce their plaited polyesters in three colours apart from white — blue, red and yellow. These are solid colour and speckled. Rational use of these for sheets, halyards and control lines can lead to a considerable improvement in deck work by easing identification. For instance, genoa halyard and sheets should all be the same colour so that the sheet trimmer will immediately grab hold of the correct halyard if any adjustment to the luff tension is required without, as so often happens, letting go of the mainsail or spinnaker halyard by mistake.

There is no logical reason why a specific colour should be used for particular applications, but as most of the rope manufacturers suggest more or less the same coding, it seems reasonable to comply with this in the interests of

77

standardization. Few skippers are likely to be lucky enough to retain the same full crew throughout the season without at least once or twice having to poach crew from another boat. In that event it is important that the stranger should switch into gear as soon as possible. The recommended code is as follows:

BLUE for headsail sheets and halyards (except where two genoa halyards are carried in which case one should be of a different colour.

RED for spinnaker sheets and halyard.

YELLOW for foreguys and other control gear, but port and starboard can be different and topping lifts on foreguys. It depends if layout is clear or confusing.

WHITE for mainsheet and halyard, also for miscellaneous applications.

The important thing is to differentiate between control lines, whose confusion might have undesirable consequences. For example, the spinnaker topping lift and foreguy should be a different colour so that the pole is not allowed to sky when the intention is to brace it down. Similarly, the vang and cunningham should be different so that the vang is not inadvertently released on rounding the weather mark when it was only intended to release the cunningham. Slab reefing systems also demand a coding pattern otherwise the wrong reefing pennant will often be tugged to no avail.

All it requires is common sense and a little planning. The trouble generally is that a yacht's ropes are virtually the last item to be considered when equipping a new boat. With a new boat an owner should specify rope at an early stage and

length should be slightly liberal, so each line can be cut to the exact requirement after trials.

British Standard 4928 covers manufacture of synthetic ropes. In this, colour dyeing is applied without weakening the rope as it is substituted for the heat treatment in the process. It is seldom satisfactory for a user to dye his own rope; certainly vivid colours are unlikely to be obtained.

Suitable sizes of rope are shown in Fig 18. Rope is now sold by its metric diameter. On page 80 is shown nearest equivalent to inches circumference, which some persons may still use when visualizing rope thickness.

## Wire for running and standing rigging

Wire is used for both running and standing rigging and the inherent difference between the wires suited to one or other is the amount of flexibility that is endowed.

For standing rigging—i.e. shrouds and stays—either rod or wire may be used. Rod is considerably more expensive and more susceptible to undetectable fatigue, but is less prone to stretch than wire. Wire used for standing rigging is normally either of $7 \times 7$ construction or $1 \times 19$. This means that in the $7 \times 7$ construction the wire rope is made up of seven strands twisted together with each of the seven strands in turn made up of seven individual wires, six of them twisted around a single wire core. The construction of $1 \times 19$ wire rope simply consists of nineteen individual wires twisted into a rope.

As far as application is concerned $1 \times 19$ is considered to be most suitable of the wire ropes for standing rigging, as it is slightly more resistant to stretch and

| Overall Yacht length ft. | Main dia mm | Jib dia mm | HALYARDS Spinnaker dia mm |
|---|---|---|---|
| 30 | 10 | 10 | 8 |
| 36 | 12 | 12 | 10 |
| 45 and over | 12 | 12 | 12 |

| Overall Yacht length ft. | Main or Jib dia mm | Genoa dia mm | SHEETS Spinnaker dia mm | Spinnaker light weather dia mm |
|---|---|---|---|---|
| 30 | 10 | 12 | 12 | 8 |
| 36 | 12 | 14 | 14 | 8 |
| 45 | 12 | 16 | 16 | 10 |

| Overall Yacht length ft. | Nylon dia mm | ANCHOR RODE Polyester dia mm | Danforth or C.Q.R. anchor kg | Chain dia | Kedge anchor nylon dia mm |
|---|---|---|---|---|---|
| 29 | 14 | 16 | 14 | 8 | 8 |
| 31 | 16 | 18 | 14 | 9 | 10 |
| 36 | 18 | 20 | 19 | 9 | 10 |
| 45 | 20 | 22 | 25 | 11 | 10 |
| 50 | 20 | 22 | 25 | 11 | 10 |
| 60 | 24 | — | 34 | 11 | 12 |

*Fig 18. Table of synthetic rope sizes for various tasks on different sized yachts.*

79

has a smoother surface, making it kinder to hands, sails and sheets. It is almost impossible to splice, but that does not matter, particularly as most wire terminals are nowadays swaged with some proprietary terminal.

Running rigging demands fairly considerable flexibility from the wire and for this reason 6 × 19 construction is normally used. This means that nineteen wires are used in each of the six strands and because of the fineness of the individual wires the construction is considerably more flexible than the others. For halyards it is normal practice to use flexible wire with a rope tail, with a long splice used to join the two parts. Nowadays the tail will usually have a plaited sheath around a polyester core. With careful workmanship the rope sheath can be extended over a few feet of the wire, so that the part of the halyard that will bear the load on the winch will be wire with the coat to protect the winch drum.

Wire can either be stainless steel or galvanized steel. Stainless steel is a little stronger and is resistant to the corrosion that galvanized wire is not. However, that does not mean that stainless steel is resistant to chafe or fatigue—in fact *stainless steel used for running rigging usually has a life expectancy of about one season or less.* A few individual wires will part and the raw ends are an indication that the wire has ceased to have uniform strength with the ultimate result that a break is fairly imminent. Galvanized wire is usually discarded on account of its corroded appearance even though it may have some serviceable life left. However, like stainless, a few strands of wire will part first and the resultant upset of the load sharing means it has to be discarded. Galvanized wire is cheaper

than stainless steel and, as it will last for running rigging as long as stainless, it is probably preferable.

For standing rigging stainless steel is usually better, as long as it is treated cautiously when the mast is being stepped or unstepped. It does not take kindly to kinking and may lose about half its strength as a result. It has the added disadvantage that it need not necessarily give tell tale signs of imminent failure as will galvanized wire. However, the resistance to corrosion means that its life expectancy is considerably greater and can usually prove to be an economy.

| Inches Circumference | Inches Diameter | MM Diameter |
|---|---|---|
| $\frac{1}{2}$ inch | 0·16 | 4 mm |
| $\frac{3}{4}$ inch | 0·24 | 6 mm |
| 1 inch | 0·32 | 8 mm |
| $1\frac{1}{4}$ inch | 0·40 | 10 mm |
| $1\frac{1}{2}$ inch | 0·48 | 12 mm |
| 2 inch | 0·64 | 16 mm |

*Nearest equivalent of rope in metric diameter to inches circumference.*

# 9. Hull and deck check list

This list of design and fitting out points is mostly based on a list originally collected by Roderick Stephens.

## Hull

1. *Steering* must be free and firm without stiffness or backlash. It is worth persisting in yardwork until this is completely right.
2. *Bilge drainage.* A tea cup of water poured in anywhere must find its way fairly quickly to the lowest part of the bilge, whence it can be pumped out.
3. Permanent *flotation marks* on centre-line fore and aft on the datum waterline and a further set twelve inches above them are useful for checking the trim at any time.
4. Propeller *shaft marking* should be provided so that the propeller can be turned to minimum resistance from inside the yacht before a race begins.
5. The propeller *shaft lock* should be a sheer pin (brass) which will lock for normal use but can be severed in an emergency. Brake systems not fully released can create a fire hazard.
6. There should be *no sharp edges* or corners in the accommodation or on deck.
7. *Bilges* with a rough finish are almost impossible to keep clean.
8. Impenetrable *interior liners* are too common in GRP boats and must be avoided.
9. *Electric switches* should be sited clear of water and spray. It is better to have to reach a bit further and have the switches work.
10. The *emergency tiller* should be fitted from time to time (swollen wood?, rusted steel?) Does it affect the compass? A strong person should then treat it very roughly, as a test!
11. *Cockpit drain guard* should be a light gauge cross, which stops potential blocking objects getting down, but offers no measurable obstruction to quick water outflow. The same applies to diaphragm pump intakes.
12. *Through hull fittings.* Sinks must not be sited low so that they take in water when heeled. *Water intakes* (toilet etc.) must be low so that they operate when heeled. The *exhaust for the engine* must be well above the waterline even when down by the stern when motoring fast, running in a seaway or heeled. *Seacocks* must be fitted on all skin fittings, be reasonable of access, turned easily by hand and marked in the 'full open' and 'full shut' positions. The *bilge pump discharge* should not be an *inward* source of water: the pipe should be looped high under the deck and dis-

## hull and deck

charge above the waterline on or near the centreline. *Fuel tank vents* should be on or near the centreline where fumes cannot be carried into the accommodation. *Water tank vents* should emerge at a sink or drain below decks where overflow when filling does not matter, yet there is no chance of salt water contamination.

### Deck and rig

1. *Sail tyers and small lines.* Plenty of these are always useful and they should be kept in marked or coloured bags which are readily accessible.

2. *Goosenecks* and kicking straps are frequently blocked by gear or fittings when the boom is squared off which can result in dangerous strains: clearance must be made where necessary.

3. *Split pins.* The pin should be cut so that below the head it is one and a half times the diameter of the clevis pin which is being secured. The ends, after cutting, should be rounded with a smooth flat file. If possible in use they should be slightly opened and not bent right back: however, depending on the fitting this may be necessary so that tape can be applied smoothly to prevent fouling. All exposed split pins should be taped everywhere on deck or in the rig. (*Cotter pin* US.)

4. *Bitter ends.* All halyards should be arranged so they can never go aloft. Ends can be tied, shackled, or stopper knots, large enough not to enter blocks or mast sheaves, made in their ends.

5. *Mast wiring.* Wiring to navigation lights on pulpits or mast should not use so-called waterproof plugs and sockets on deck; these are invariably swamped, shorted and corroded. Wires should pass through the deck using watertight glands, which can be very tight, and then connect to main supply below deck as high up as possible. Where a mast is stepped to the keel, wiring is sometimes damaged when the mast is

unstepped. A good arrangement is a longitudinal hole that permits disconnected wires to be lodged inside when the mast is being moved. These wires are fished out when required to be connected and taken to their various hook-up points (not close to the mast partners).

6. *Lubrication.* An oil can should be kept within reach and used frequently on all moving gear (spinnaker pistons, goose neck track, metal cam jammers, snap shackles etc.) on deck. Otherwise salt water will jam many fittings tight.

7. *Boatswain's chair.* A boat that does not carry one cannot expect to repair or adjust anything more than about ten feet above the deck. You might as well have the engine compartment sealed in a power boat! The strops must be short, so that when the chair shackle is two blocks, the man aloft is within reach of the masthead. The hoist should have a metal ring of such gauge that it will take any halyard shackle in use. The seat should be smooth but not varnished and, as is well known, the strops must be spliced below it, so that if it breaks the user is still supported by them.

8. *Halyard noise.* It must be possible despite leads and splices, for all halyards to be taken clear of the mast and still be secured, so that they will not tap the mast when the boat is left in her berth.

9. *Storm jib.* This must have been hoisted, sheeted and lowered, preferably in a good breeze which will show any defects in its function. The deck is usually laid out ideally for genoas, but sometimes difficulties can arise with jibs. This is particularly

so for (a) *effective deck leads*, (snatch blocks can burst open, does the jib lead inside the shrouds, or outside like a genoa?), (b) *head spans* (are there extra pieces to fit a groove), (c) *emergency hanking* by lacing when the groove is not usable and (d) whether *special sheets* should be available (genoa sheets are unnecessarily long for jibs).

# 10. Winches

Though many types of yacht use halyard and sheet winches, it is clear that the major manufacturers design their products for ocean racing boats—which is an advantage.

The rules governing winches are those which allow manual power only and forbid sheet winches to be operated below decks. There are some fundamental rules for siting; if riding turns and other difficulties are experienced on an existing yacht, check if these hints are being disregarded.

1. Being circular, the horizontal approach angle is immaterial, but the vertical should be between 95° and 120° to the axis of the drum. (Fig 19.)
2. Footblocks (turning blocks) may have to be installed to give a suitable lead, but are a potential point of high loading and should be avoided if possible. (Fig 20.)
3. There is a position where maximum power can be applied by the human body. An important factor is the height of the winch handle above the feet of the winder. This is shown in Fig 21 to be best at around 2 ft 6 in.
4. Apart from these basics, the winder must be physically comfortable when winding and the handle clear of lifelines, low main boom, mainsheet etc. A winch in use to leeward, canted out will be approaching horizontal when the yacht is heavily heeled.

## Choosing the right winch

The accompanying table (Fig 22) lists the winches of three of the largest manufacturers and is a guide to winch suitability for a given job. But it is only a guide because it should be appreciated that there are a great many considerations before deciding which winch to buy. It will depend on the sail area, the configuration of the deck, specifically who will sail it (will it be a full racing crew or a family team?). Each case has to be treated on its own merits and generally the winch manufacturers are only too pleased to advise an owner on the correct choice for any specific application.

Strangely, a cruising yacht requires as much, if not more, thought about its winches than a racing boat. Almost invariably the cruiser will also need more powerful winches than the equivalent on a racing yacht. First of all there is usually less muscle on a cruising yacht and secondly technique will probably be lacking. It's all very well holding the attitude that a cruising man has all the time in the world but the reality of the situation is that the longer it takes to sheet in a sail the greater the energy that will be required, and not just because more time

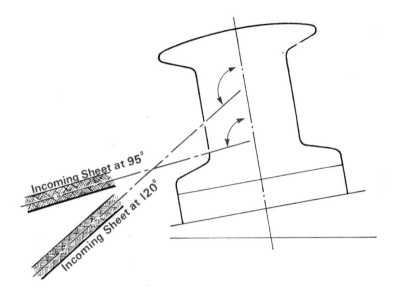

*Fig 19. A sheet should lead into a winch at an angle of between 90° and 120° to the vertical axis. Angles beyond these will cause riding turns.*

is spent on the job. Whereas a sharp racing crew will have a sail sheeted in almost before it has started drawing, the cruising man will be endeavouring to grind in a fully loaded sheet. In such a situation one powerful winch properly positioned will be better than two smaller winches. Time lost in swopping over sheets on a single winch will be negligible when compared with the very real gains in winding efficiency.

### Maintenance

To quote one winch maker 'unfortunately certain manufacturers have publicized the concept that maintenance may be carried out by pouring buckets of water over the winch. In our experience this would do little other than give you a pair of rather wet feet'.

A winch is no different from any other mechanical apparatus—it needs regular attention to maintain its proper working

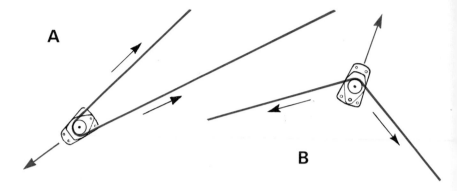

Fig 20. Where footblock leads double back there will be increased loads on the deck fitting. Therefore such blocks should not be used unless completely necessary. A shows how load is nearly doubled, but at B strains are much less.

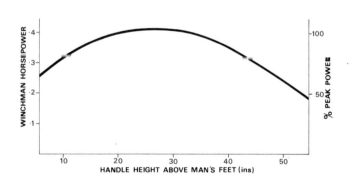

Fig 21. Optimum distance between handle and feet of winch winder is shown by this graph.

order. Some winch manufacturers issue service manuals and provided the instructions given are followed diligently there is no reason why a winch should not give years of efficient service. (eg. Lewmar Marine issue a maintenance manual covering every winch, primarily intended for boatyards with instructions on dismantling, fitting spares, maintenance and lubricants. They also publish *How to use your Lewmar winch*, a more consumer orientated booklet with brief but fully illustrated instructions for stripping and cleaning each type of winch. Barient issues a *Maintenance and Service Manual*.)

On an average cruising yacht or cruiser-racer with five or six winches, if one winch were stripped, cleaned and lubricated every week, making it in effect a six-week cycle, they should remain in a healthy working condition. All the parts should be removed carefully according to the service manual and placed on a rag. Old lubricant should be wiped off with tissue or ideally soaked in kerosene or other petroleum solvent until the previous lubricant has been removed. All parts should then be re-greased, either with proprietary winch lubricants (e.g. Lewmar grease 7385) or such commonly available greases as Castrol LM. However, grease should be applied sparingly as any excess may tend to restrict the free action of moving parts because of its viscosity—pawls, for instance, can tend to jam shut and thus encourage the winch to backspin under load.

On thoroughbred racing yachts where a dedicated crew may be prepared to spend more time on odd jobs than the average weekend sailor, light engineering oils should be used as a lubricant in preference to grease, as its lower frictional properties promises smoother and more reliable action. However, it must be stressed that then every winch should be stripped and oiled before every race as the oil will tend to run off the parts very quickly.

It hardly needs stating that the guts of the winch should be inspected for wear—bits of swarf in the winch will be indicative of abrasion somewhere.

Tools required for routine servicing:
Large and small screwdriver or knife blade.
Allen keys
Non-fluffy cloth.
Light machine oil.
Suitable grease (as mentioned above).
Cleaning fluid or gasoline (for washing off old grease)
For full stripping more tools are required. On reel winches take care *not to apply lubricant on or near brake drums.*

*Fig 22. (Next page) Winch sizes recommended from three major manufacturers of sheet and halyard winches to offshore boats.*

87

# CHART OF RECOMMENDED WINCHES

| BOAT SIZE (up to) | | 22 FT miniton | 25 FT ¼ ton | | 30 FT ½ ton | | 34 FT ¾ ton | | 38 FT 1 ton | | 44 FT 2 ton | | 48 FT | | 54 FT | | 60 FT | | 65 FT | | 70 FT | |
|---|---|---|---|---|---|---|---|---|---|---|---|---|---|---|---|---|---|---|---|---|---|---|
| RELATIVE SAIL AREA | | S | S | L | S | L | S | L | S | L | S | L | S | L | S | L | S | L | S | L | S | L |
| GENOA SHEET | BARIENT | 9 | 10 | 16 | 21 | 22 | 26 | 28 | 28 | 28 | 32 | 32 | 35 | 35 | XII | XII | XII | XII | XII | XVII | XVII | XVII |
| | BARLOW | 16 | 18 | 22 | 24 | 24 | 26 | 28 | 28 | 28 | 32 | 32 | 34 | 34 | 34 | 34 | Grinder | Grinder | Grinder | Grinder | Grinder | Grinder |
| | LEWMAR | 7 | 8 | 16 | 25 | 40 | 43 | 44 | 44 | 48 or 55 | 55 | 65 | 65 | 80 | 94 | 95 | 95 | 96 | 96 | 96 | 96 | 96 |
| SPINNAKER SHEET | BARIENT | 9 | 10 | 10 | 16 | 16 | 21 | 22 | 22 | 26 | 28 | 32 | 32 | 32 | 32 | 35 | 35 | 35 | 35 | 36 | 36 | 36 |
| | BARLOW | 15 | 16 | 16 | 18 | 18 | 22 | 22 | 26 | 26 | 28 | 28 | 32 | 32 | 32 | 32 | 34 | 34 | 36 | 36 | 36 | 36 |
| | LEWMAR | 6 | 7 | 8 | 10 | 16 | 25 | 40 | 40 | 43 | 44 | 48 | 48 | 55 | 55 | 65 | 65 | 65 | 65 | 65 | 65 | 65 |
| MAIN SHEET | BARIENT | | 10 | 10 | 10 | 10 | 16 | 16 | 18 | 18 | 18 | 18 | 23 ST | 23 ST | 27 ST | 27 ST | 28 ST | 28 ST | 32 ST | 32 ST | 32 ST | 32 ST |
| | BARLOW | | | 16 | 16 | 16 | 16 | 16 | 16 | 16 | 18 | 18 | 24 | 24 | 24 | 24 | 28 | 28 | 30 | 30 | 32 | 32 |
| | LEWMAR | | 6 | 8 | 8 | 8 | 16 | 16 | 25 | 25 | 40 | 40 | 43 | 43 | 44 | 44 | 44 | 44 | 48 | 48 | 48 | 48 |
| GENOA HALYARD | BARIENT | 9 | 10 | 10 | 18 | 18 | 18 | 18 | 21 | 22 | 22 | 22 | 28 | 28 | 32 | 32 | 32 | 35 | 35 | 35 | 35 | 35 |
| | BARLOW | 15H | 16 | 16 | 18 | 18 | 22 | 22 | 24 | 26 | 28 | 28 | 30 | 30 | 30 | 30 | 32 | 34 | 34 | 34 | 36 | 36 |
| | LEWMAR | 6 | 8 | 16 | 25 | 25 | 40 | 40 | 40 | 43 | 43 | 44 | 48 | 48 | 55 | 55 | 65 | 65 | 65 | 65 | 65 | 65 |
| SPINNAKER HALYARD | BARIENT | 9 | 10 | 10 | 16 | 16 | 16 | 18 | 21 | 21 | 22 | 22 | 26 | 26 | 28 | 28 | 28 | 30 | 32 | 32 | 32 | 32 |
| | BARLOW | 15H | 15 | 16 | 16 | 16 | 16 | 16 | 22 | 22 | 26 | 26 | 26 | 26 | 28 | 28 | 30 | 30 | 32 | 32 | 34 | 34 |

| | C1 | C2 | C3 | C4 | C5 | C6 | C7 | C8 | C9 | C10 | C11 | C12 | C13 | C14 | C15 | C16 | C17 | C18 | C19 | C20 | C21 | C22 | |
|---|---|---|---|---|---|---|---|---|---|---|---|---|---|---|---|---|---|---|---|---|---|---|---|
| MAIN HALYARD | 6 | 6 | 7 | 8 | 16 | 16 | 25 | 25 | 40 | 43 | 43 | 43 | 44 | 48 | 48 | 48 | 55 | 55 | 55 | 55 | 55 | 55 | LEWMAR |
| | 9 | 9 | 10 | 10 | 10 | 10 | 18 | 18 | 18 | 21 | 22 | 26 | 26 | 26 | 26 | 28 | 28 | 28 | 32 | 32 | 32 | 32 | BARIENT |
| | 15H | 15H | 16 | 16 | 2H | 2H | 4H | 4H | 5H | 5H | 6H | 6H | 6H | 6H | 8H | 8H | 8H | 10H | 10H | 10H | 10H | 10H | BARLOW |
| | 6 | 6 | 6 | 7 | 8 | 8 | 10 | 10 | 16 | 25 | 40 or 1H | 40or2H | 40or2·2H | 43or2·2H | 44or3H | 44or3H | 48 or 3H | 48 or 3H | 48 or 3H | 48 or 3H | 48 or 3H | 48 or 3H | LEWMAR |
| TOPPING LIFT | | | | | | | | | 10 | 10 | 21 | 23ST | 23ST | 23ST | 27ST | 27ST | 27ST | 27ST | 27ST | 27ST | 28ST | 28ST | BARIENT |
| | | | | 16 | 16 | 16 | 16 | 18 | 18 | 22 | 22 | 22 | 24 | 24 | 26 | 26 | 28 | 28 | 30 | 30 | 32 | 32 | BARLOW |
| | | | | | | 7 | 8 | 8 | 10 | 10 | 16 or 25 | 25 | 40 | 40 | 40 | 43 | 43 | 43 | 43 | 43 | 43 | 43 | LEWMAR |
| FORE-GUY | | | | 6 | 6 | 7 | 8 | 10 | 10 | 16 | 21 | 23ST | 23ST | 23ST | 27ST | 27ST | 27ST | 27ST | 28ST | 28ST | 28ST | 28ST | BARIENT |
| | 6 | 6 | 7 | 8 | 10 | 10 | 16 | 16 | 25 | 25 | 40 | 40 | 40 | 43 | 43 | 43 | 44 | 44 | 44 | 44 | 44 | 44 | LEWMAR |
| REEF | | | | | 6 | 6 | 6 | 9 | 10 | 16 | 16 | 21 | 23ST | 23ST | 27ST | 27ST | 27ST | 28ST | 28ST | 28ST | 28ST | 28ST | BARIENT |
| | 6 | | | | 6 | 6 | 6 | 7 | 8 | 16 | 25 | 25 | 40 | 40 | 43 | 43 | 44 | 48 | 48 | 48 | 48 | 48 | LEWMAR |

# 11. Pre- and post-race checklists

**Pre-race checklist**
A. at dock    B. on way to race
C. before starting gun

A. Navigator—study tides and sailing instructions.
A. Ascertain that all sails are properly packed and that they are accessible in the order that will most likely be required.
A. Ensure that winches, snap shackles, spinnaker pole end fittings and all other mechanical parts are fully operational. (e.g. have been lubricated.)
A. Hoist racing flag and appropriate code or class flag.
A. Check time.
A. Check wind instruments that they are operational.

C. If possible sail boat on parallel course with the first leg to effect correct sail luff tensions.

B. Check that the genoa sheet lead position is correct and that the sheet is properly lead.
B. Ensure that the spinnaker sheets and guys are properly lead.
B. Lower log impeller.
B. Check sails against black bands.

C. Check propeller alignment, after stopping engine, for minimum sailing resistance.
C. Set backstay tension for first leg.

## Post race checklist

Did the boat touch bottom during the race or was any damage inflicted that might require attention?

Is all the running rigging—sheets, guys and halyards—free of chafe? Were any sails torn or damaged in any way that might require attention?

Is the bottom clean enough for the next race or will it need scrubbing?

Is the standing rigging properly set up for the next race—correct shroud tension, etc?

Are all the terminal fittings operable, snap shackles properly lubricated etc?

Are all the winches and turning blocks operable? Do they require stripping and lubricating?

Was any item of equipment lost or broken that might require replacing—winch handles, snatch blocks etc?

Do the batteries require charging? Are all the navigation lights, instruments and cabin lights functioning?

Do the charts require drying out? Are the correct charts aboard for the next race? Has the tidal situation for the next race been established? Are the correct flags aboard for the next race?

Is there adequate fuel and water aboard? Has the crew been informed of the arrangements for the next race—time of departure to allow adequate time to get to the starting line and to tune up before the gun?

Has any food that will not stay fresh been cleared out? Have food and refreshment arrangements for the next race been made? If any chores have to be carried out by the crew before the next race do they have the full information they require?

Do the sails require drying out?

Has the racing flag been removed?

Has the backstay been eased off?

Are all the ventilators open?

Have the log impellers been retracted?

Are the bilges dry?

Have the seacocks and isolating power switches been turned off?

# 12. Life-jackets and harnesses

Every type of vessel from small dinghy to ocean freighter carries the personal emergency gear of life-jackets (life preservers, US). In addition offshore racers and cruisers carry crew harnesses. Both types of equipment need care, and maintenance, as well as regular checking for condition.

## Nomenclature (UK)

Life-jackets on an offshore boat should comply with British Standard 3595. (This will be marked on them.) They are supplied by the owner and kept in good condition for emergency. They are not for continuous wearing where they could become chafed and damaged. 'Buoyancy aids' are something different: intended for dinghy sailing as an aid to swimming and clinging to a capsized boat. Such aids are sometimes worn on offshore boats by individuals, but are an addition to the ship's life-jackets. ORC special regulations 11.1 and 11.2 refer.

## Care of life-jackets

1. When brought on board remove wrapping, polythene etc. Fit whistle and water-light if not already attached.
2. Check frequently for inflation retention by blowing up hard and leaving for some hours. Condemn (or return to manufacturers) any which do not remain inflated hard. They have probably perished.
3. Return life-jackets for annual service to manufacturer. Some jackets are supplied with vouchers for this purpose.

## British Standard 3595

The British Standard has more than twenty pages of specifications which have been developed since 1963, so life-jackets to this standard can be regarded with considerable confidence. Among the most important assets of BSS life-jackets are:

1. Minimum buoyancy of 35 pounds (adults) and 20 pounds (small children).
2. Distribution of buoyancy so that the mouth of exhausted or unconscious person is held clear of water and trunk of body inclined between 30° and 60° from vertical. If the person has fallen in the water or floats initially face downwards the jacket has to 'self-right' him into the desired position.
3. A becket to enable lifting out without damage to jacket.
4. Materials are rot proof, have minimum tear strength, have to be heat cured, copper resistant, diesel fuel resistant, have low flammability and resist fresh and salt water at an extreme range of temperatures.

## Nomenclature (US Coast Guard-approved Life Preservers)

In the United States, the Coast Guard refers to life preservers as Personal Flotation Devices (PFD's) and distinguishes five types:

*Type I:* Designed to turn an unconscious person from a face-down position in the water to an upright or tipped slightly backward position. The required minimum buoyancy for an adult size is 22 pounds and for a child size 11 pounds. Recommended for offshore and ocean sailing where a person might have to remain in the water for a long period of time.

*Type II:* Designed for the same purpose as Type I, but of lighter buoyancy (minimum 15½ pounds for adult size and 7 pounds for a young child's size). Recommended for inshore sailing.

*Type III:* Designed to keep a conscious person in an upright position or tipped slightly backward. Same buoyancy requirements as Type II, but has a smaller turning moment and affords greater wearing comfort. Recommended for sailing close inshore or on lakes.

*Type IV:* Designed to be thrown to a person in the water. Minimum buoyancy of 16½ pounds.

*Type V:* Wearable devices designed for a particular and limited purpose. Requirements vary.

Many kinds of PFD's are currently manufactured. The following table, prepared by the Coast Guard, classifies the most common kinds according to equivalent performance types.

Performance Type I PFD

| Number on label | Devices marked |
|---|---|
| 160.002 | Life preserver |
| 160.003 | Life preserver |
| 160.004 | Life preserver |
| 160.005 | Life preserver |
| 160.055 | Life preserver |

Performance Type II PFD

| | |
|---|---|
| 160.047 | Buoyant vest |
| 160.052 | Buoyant vest |
| 160.060 | Buoyant vest |

Performance Type IV PFD

| | |
|---|---|
| 160.048 | Buoyant cushion |
| 160.049 | Buoyant cushion |
| 160.050 | Ring life buoy |
| 160.009 | Ring life buoy |

Performance Type V PFD

| | |
|---|---|
| 160.053 | Work vest |
| 160.064 | Special purpose |

A device intended to be worn may be equivalent to Type II or Type III. A device that is equivalent to Type III is marked 'Type III Device—may not turn unconscious wearer.' A device intended to be grasped is equivalent to Type IV.

## US PFD requirements for different boats

All the PFD's carried on any boat must be Coast Guard approved, in good condition, of a suitable size for the intended wearer, and readily accessible. Boats under 16 feet (including canoes and kayaks) must have one PFD (of Type I, II, III, or IV) for each person aboard.

## life-saving gear

Boats 16 feet or larger must have one life-jacket or vest (of Type I, II, or III) for each person, plus one throwable (Type IV) device.

The American Boat and Yacht Council has life preserver standards similar to the Coast Guard's, but unlike the Coast Guard requirements the ABYC's recommendations are not enforced by law. The ABYC's life preserver standards are included in their book *Safety Standards for Small Craft*, which provides a large amount of information pertaining to all aspects of boating safety. The book is published in loose-leaf form and so is easy to keep up-to-date. To obtain a copy, write to the ABYC, 15 East 26 Street, New York, NY 10010. The current cost is $25.00.

### Harnesses

As for life-jackets there should be enough on board for all the crew. They should be checked regularly for chafe on the lines and seizings and wear of the webbing straps. Hinges on hooks need oiling from time to time. Harnesses are invariably worn in bad weather and these tend to salt stain and corrosion, as weather improves they are thankfully pushed soaking wet into a locker below; hence the need for maintenance.

There is a British Standard 4224, but most harnesses in use do not comply with it. It has a number of requirements including breaking strain of line 4560 lbs, non-magnetic fittings stainless or plated, self closing hooks to close round a bar of $\frac{1}{2}$ in. (Fig 23.)

Some crew members may have safety harnesses built into foul weather jackets. This obviates one of the most difficult points of a harness, which is getting it on and off without a struggle. The deck should be surveyed to make sure there are adequate 'hook-on' points. Two or more men hooked on to the same lifeline is not advisable. Jackstays along the deck, on which the harness carbine hook slides, are seldom the answer and sheets, vangs etc are invariably fouled. The experienced crewman judges when to hook on and when not: to be able to do this the harness must, of course, be on him in anything except light weather.

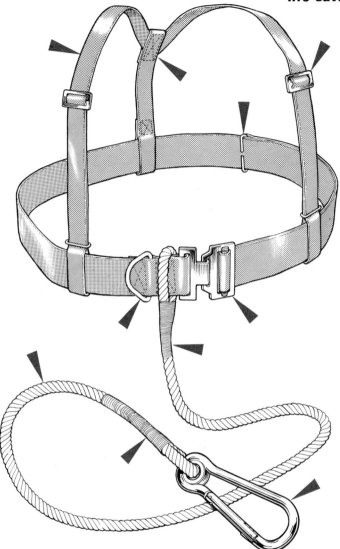

*Fig 23. Important elements in the construction of a safety harness (some of these particulars are guided by BS 4224). Braces with a minimum width of $\frac{3}{4}$ in. Fittings. Able to go round $\frac{1}{2}$ in diameter cylinder; line cannot disengage from them because thimble set in hook. Rope. Three strand dacron/terylene, minimum diameter $\frac{1}{2}$ in., minimum breaking load 5000 lb with splices of four full tucks and two taper tucks. Webbing. Lock stitched with rot proof thread, thread no closer to edge than $\frac{1}{8}$ in. Minimum breaking load of material 2500 lb per inch.*

# 13. Radio telephony

## Radio telephony

Three types of transmitter are suitable for sailing yachts.

1. MF/HF radio telephone, single side band (SSB) (Double side band is now obsolescent internationally and may not be installed).
2. VHF radio telephone.
3. Single or multi-frequency emergency transmitters. These broadcast only on distress frequencies 2182 kHz for shipping or 121.5 and 243 MHz for civil and military aircraft.

MF/HF RT has greater range (up to 400 miles) than VHF, but is more expensive, heavier, bulkier, requires skill in tuning, uses more electric power, but can transmit on the marine distress frequency (2182 kHz).

An ocean racer in coastal waters (or indeed making an ocean crossing) can well carry VHF together with a single frequency emergency transmitter. The latter either takes speech so that MAYDAY can be spoken into it, or broadcasts the international two-tone distress frequency. It is assumed a medium/long wave receiver for broadcast stations would also be carried.

## VHF radio

*Installation*

Usually a 12 volt supply is required and the power supply should be connected direct to battery and not through the isolating switch for all other ship's equipment. Aerial position should be at masthead because VHF is fundamentally 'line-of-sight' and VHF aerials can be short, thin and with little weight and windage. In the event of dismasting there should be a properly prepared reserve aerial which can be plugged into the set. Typical weight of a set is between 5 and 10 lb. Sets are not much bigger than some domestic receivers.

*Main uses (UK) (For US see page 105)*

1. Connection to post office telephone network through authorized coast radio stations (Channels 23 to 28 and others).
2. Port operations (Channels 12 and 14 and others)
3. Ship-to-ship (Channels 6 and 8 and others)
4. Ship-to-Coastguard (Channel 67. A search and rescue frequency not for routine messages).
5. Distress (Channel 16). UK coastguards keep watch on Channel 16, ships usually keep watch on this channel.
6. Ship-to-club or yacht harbour (Channel 37. For maritime messages and not for messages to third parties).

*Fig 24. UK Post Office coastal stations which can communicate on VHF radio telephony.*

SHETLAND

WICK

STONEHAVEN

CLYDE

CULLERCOATS

PORTPATRICK

ANGLESEY

HUMBER

CELTIC

SEVERN

THAMES
NORTH
FORELAND

HASTINGS

NITON

LANDS END

START POINT

# radio telephony

## Licences and RT procedure in UK

Licences are required for a radio set on a ship whether it is a transmitter, receiver only or emergency transmitter. These 'ship licences' are issued by the Home Office, Radio Regulatory Division, Waterloo Road, London SE1 8UA.

VHF may only be used by a person holding, as a minimum qualification, the Restricted Certificate of Competence. Application forms for the examination for this are issued by the Post Office, External Telecommunications Executive, Maritime Radio Services Department, Union House, St. Martin's-le-Grand, London EC1A 1AR.

Usually a person from the Ship Radio Inspection Office of the Department of Trade at a nearby port will go to the yacht and inspect the installation and test the owner (or other applicants) if he does not yet hold a certificate, at the same time.

## RT procedure. (VHF)

Most sets installed in yachts are 'simplex' equipment. When transmitting it is not possible to hear other stations. The use of 'over' at the end of a transmission therefore indicates that the sender has released the transmit button on his microphone and is inviting the other station to send. Coast stations and most commercial stations are equipped with duplex equipment and so can hear interruptions etc. No special action is required by the yacht user.

*Few yachts will be on listening watch, so after the set is switched on listen to check that the frequency is clear, before starting to send.* All calls are initiated on Channel 16.

Procedure is best illustrated by examples, the simplest being ship-to-ship. The yacht *Shark* is calling *Whale*.

98

*Shark transmits*
(on Channel 16)
Hello, Whale. This is Shark.
This is Shark. Over

*Whale transmits*
(on Channel 16)

Hello, Shark. This is Whale. This is
Whale. Over

Hello, Whale, this is Shark.
Channel 6. Over

This is Whale. Channel 6. Going now
Over

(Both switch to Channel 6)
(Channel 6)
The initial caller always speaks first on
the new Channel.

Hello Whale. We are still making
good progress and (etc) (message
continues) Over

(on Channel 6)
At the end of the conversation both parties
use 'out' eg.

This is Whale. Thanks for all the
information. Let's try same time
tomorrow. Good sailing. Out.

*The word 'Hello'* may be dropped once
communication is established. For transmissions not on VHF, procedure is
slightly different; for instance station
names can be repeated up to three times.

*To call a coast radio station (CRS) for
linking to the telephone system*, the
following procedure is used. The coast
station will need to know accurately
the yacht's call-sign and name in order to
record telephone charges.

*Shark transmits*
(on Channel 16)
Hello Lewis radio, this is Shark.
This is Shark. Can I have a link call
please? Over

# radio telephony

*Lewis (coast) radio transmits*
(on Channel 16)
Hello Shark. This is Lewis radio.
Channel 28. Stand by. Over

Hello Lewis. This is Shark.
Channel 28. Going now. Over
(on Channel 28)

(on Channel 28)
Hello Shark. This is Lewis Radio.
Please give me your call sign and spell
your vessel's name. Over

Lewis. Shark. Call sign
2 NGS. Shark is S-H-A-R-K
Over

Shark. What is the number you want?
Over

Lewis. Shark. I want
01-953-4241. Over

Shark. Thank you. Stand by.

(The yacht waits while the number is
obtained)

Hello Shark. This is Lewis. Your
number is on the line; go ahead. Over.

(*Shark* then speaks immediately to his
correspondent)
Hello. This is George Brown on the
yacht Shark. Is that Larry Smith. Over.

(through coast station)
Hello George. Yes Larry here.
I thought you might . . . (etc)

At the end of the call the coast radio
operator tells the calling vessel the time
and the price of the call and then closes
the conversation.

100

*Example when station called has not
heard the name of the calling station.*

*Shark transmits*
(Channel 16)
Hello Lewis Radio. This is Shark.
This is Shark. Can I have a link call,
please? Over.

(no reply)

*Lewis radio transmits*
(Channel 16)

Hello Lewis Radio. This is Shark.
This is Shark. Over

Station calling Lewis Radio. This
is Lewis Radio. Say again. Over.

Hello Lewis Radio (etc)

To avoid crowding of Channel 16,
authority may soon be given to initiate
calls on working frequencies. This is
already done in USA (see page 108).

*Terms used on RT*
'Roger' means received and understood.
('Roger' is from a long out-dated phonetic
alphabet and 'Romeo' is recommended
by some authorities)

'Wait' indicates no reply expected while
station finds something out, obtains
link call etc. and will then return with a
further message.
'Out' indicates the conversation is being
closed. Both stations involved end with
it.
'Wilco' means 'I understand what you
are saying and will comply with it.
'Say again' is used when repetition is
required (*not* 'repeat')

A list of terms is shown in *Standard Marine
Navigational Vocabulary (Merchant
Shipping Notice M767*—Department of
Trade (UK))

## Distress and safety

Other important RT terms concern distress and safety as follows. These are used on Channel 16 on VHF (as well as 2182 kHz on MF)

Bearings are always expressed in 360 degree rotation from North (true unless otherwise stated). Bearing is always *from mark to ship.*

MAYDAY is the international distress call for immediate assistance.

PAN PAN is the international urgency signal for messages which concern the safety of the ship and individuals (e.g. medical cases, damage to vessel but no immediate distress).

SECURITE is the international safety signal for urgent navigational and meteorological warnings.

MAYDAY has priority over all other traffic.

PAN has priority over all traffic except MAYDAY.

1. All stations hearing MAYDAY must abandon other transmissions and listen.
2. Coast radio station or CG answer first.
3. If no shore station responds ships in vicinity should answer the MAYDAY, but avoid interfering with each other.
4. Ships and stations further away allow ships in the vicinity to answer first.

Example where *Shark* is in distress

*Shark transmits*
(Channel 16)
MAYDAY MAYDAY MAYDAY. This is *Shark, Shark, Shark.* MAYDAY *Shark* 4 miles due south of Beachy Head. engine room fire. spreading fast will fire distress rockets. Over.
(Add type of assistance required if not obvious)

102

*Shark transmits*
(on Channel 16)

*Whale transmits*
(Channel 16)
MAYDAY. *Shark.* This is Whale.
Whale. Whale. Received MAYDAY.
Over.

Conversation can continue with the word MAYDAY prefixing all messages.

*It may be necessary to relay* a distress message: for instance *Whale* hears the message and no one else appears to have, so her operator relays it further.

*Whale transmits*
(Channel 16)
MAYDAY RELAY. MAYDAY RELAY.
MAYDAY RELAY. This is Whale. This is
Whale. This is Whale.
MAYDAY. *Shark* 4 miles due south
of Beachy Head. Shark has engine
room fire, spreading fast.
Shark will fire distress signals. Over.

*Hastings radio*
(Channel 16)
MAYDAY Whale
This is Hastings Radio. Received
MAYDAY RELAY. Over.

MAYDAY. Hastings Radio. This is
Whale. I am proceeding to
position of Shark. Over.

MAYDAY. Whale. This is Hastings
Roger. Out.
(Coast radio station will alert emergency
services, coastguard etc.)

103

# radio telephony

*Example of urgency signal.*

*Shark transmits*
(Channel 16)
PAN-PAN, PAN-PAN, PAN-PAN,
Hello all stations. Hello all stations.
Hello all stations. This is Shark,
Shark, Shark. Dismasted three
miles south of Beachy Head. Engine
out of action. Am endeavouring to
make for Newhaven. Over.

*Coastguard answers*
(Channel 16)
Hello Shark. This is Beachy
Head Coastguard. Roger.
Please repeat your position. Over.

(Contact now made with coastguard.
Other stations can resume normal traffic,
after *Shark* and coastguard have
conversed).

For all spelling on RT the international
phonetic alphabet must be learned and
used.

| | | | |
|---|---|---|---|
| A | ALFA | N | NOVEMBER |
| B | BRAVO | O | OSCAR |
| C | CHARLIE | P | PAPA |
| D | DELTA | Q | QUEBEC |
| E | ECHO | R | ROMEO |
| F | FOXTROT | S | SIERRA |
| G | GOLF | T | TANGO |
| H | HOTEL | U | UNIFORM |
| I | INDIA | V | VICTOR |
| J | JULIET | W | WHISKY |
| K | KILO | X | X-RAY |
| L | LIMA | Y | YANKEE |
| M | MIKE | Z | ZULU |

## Other services

VHF can also be used for sending radio telegrams. Contact is made with the coast station and then a telegram sent in the prescribed form.

The coast station will link the yacht without charge to a doctor or hospital for urgent medical advice.

The coast station will link the yacht to national or local meteorological offices for weather information. There are weather bulletins twice a day on VHF from most coast radio stations.

Reference books: The following official handbooks are useful for radio communication used in British yachts.

*Admiralty list of radio signals Volume I* NP 275(1) (Coast radio stations general regulations). *Vol III* NP 275(3) Meteorological services, codes, etc. *Vol VI* NP 275(6) Post radio stations and pilot vessels.

*Post Office Handbook for Radio Operators* (HMSO) (Procedure, examinations, code letters). This is required to be carried on board.

Issued at intervals by the Post Office *Notice to Ship Wireless Stations* (Obtainable from address on page 98).

## Radiotelephone licensing in the US

Although radiotelephone equipment is not mandatory on recreational boats in the United States, many boats do carry it. To install and operate radiotelephone equipment, a boat owner must obtain both a station license and an operator's license from the Federal Communications Commission (FCC).

### 1. Station Licenses

Applications for a radiotelephone station license are available from any local office of the Federal Communications Commission. The entire transaction can be completed by mail, unless you want a temporary permit allowing immediate use of the equipment. In that case, go to the FCC office in person and ask for an interim station license (good for six months) when filing the application for the full-term license. A full-term license is usually issued for a period of five years and must be displayed at all times near the radiotelephone station on the boat. An application for renewal must be filed at least thirty days before the license expires. If you sell your boat or stop operating the station for some other reason during the term of your license, be sure to return the license to the secretary of the FCC in Washington, D.C. Otherwise you will continue to be responsible for any violations.

### 2. Operator's Licenses

Except in emergencies, a person without a valid license may not operate radiotelephone equipment. (Under the supervision of an authorized operator, however, anyone can speak over a radiotelephone provided they comply with FCC regulations.) To obtain an operator's license, a person must be familiar with all of the

# radio telephony

FCC rules regarding proper radiotelephone use. Applications are available from any local office of the FCC. Like a station license, an operator's license must always be displayed near the boat's radiotelephone equipment.

## Radiotelephone operating procedures in the US

The operating procedures for radiotelephones are much the same in the United States as in the United Kingdom, although some special information applies.

### 1. Emergency Communications

*Emergency frequencies.* The two frequencies designated for emergency use are 2182 kHz in the MF band, and 156·8 MHz (Channel 16) in the VHF band. Boats with radiotelephone equipment should keep listening watches on these frequencies when their receivers are turned on but are not being used for communications on some other channel. If you are in serious danger and get no answer on the distress frequency, switch to any other channel until you make contact.

*Distress call and message.* (For very serious and immediate dangers only.) Use the radiotelephone alarm signal if available for thirty to sixty seconds in order to help attract attention. Then proceed with the distress call; MAYDAY (see page 102). For PAN PAN and SECURITE messages see page 104).

### 2. Nonemergency Communications

*Calling on a distress frequency.* Because most people maintain a listening watch on the distress frequency, this channel may also be used for calling and answering before switching to an agreed

upon working frequency. But be sure to get off the distress frequency as quickly as possible.

*Working Frequencies.* The following frequencies in the VHF 156–162 MHz band are presently designated for working use by recreational boats in the United States: 156.450 and 156.425 MHz (Channels 09 and 68): INTERSHIP and SHIP-TO-COAST. These are mainly commercial working frequencies, but they are also used by recreational boats for communication with public marinas and docks as well as with commercial vessels.

156.475, 156.575, and 156.925 MHz (Channels 69, 71, and 78): SHIP-TO-COAST. Working frequencies for recreational boats only. Used for communication with marinas, yacht clubs, and supply facilities on shore.

156.525 and 156.625 MHz (Channels 70 and 72): INTERSHIP. Working frequencies for recreational boats only. Wide number of uses.

Designated working frequencies for recreational boats in the MF band vary, depending upon the particular area of the United States. The authorized uses of MF frequencies are quite strictly controlled because of the large number of MF radiotelephone stations in the US. *For nonemergency communications, VHF should always be used before FM.*

*Making a nonemergency call.* After listening to make sure the frequency is not in use, switch to transmit and give the name and call sign of the station you are calling. Then say THIS IS, followed by your own boat's name and call sign. If there is no response, wait two minutes or more before attempting to reach the station again. If you do not make contact after the third try, wait fifteen minutes or more before your next call. When you make contact and you are on a distress frequency, agree on a working channel and switch to it as soon as possible. Keep the communication brief, no more than three minutes. When the exchange is over, sign off with your call sign. You must then wait at least ten minutes before communicating with the same station again.

*3. Communications through a public radiotelephone service*
*Types of public radiotelephone services.*
Through public radiotelephone services a boat can make calls to or receive calls from any telephone on land or sea or in the air. There are three kinds of public radiotelephone services in the United States, each working in different frequencies. Together, they offer complete coverage for the yachtsman whatever his position at sea.
VHF-FM Service
The VHF-FM service is short range, no more than twenty to fifty miles. The FCC requires boats to use this service whenever they are within the maximum distance. VHF-FM uses frequencies between 157 and 162 MHz (Channels 24 to 28 and 84 to 87). They are:

| Channel<br>number | Frequencies (MHz)<br>Transmit | Receive |
|---|---|---|
| 24 | 157.200 | 161.800 |
| 25 | 157.250 | 161.850 |
| 26 | 157.300 | 161.900 |
| 27 | 157.350 | 161·950 |
| 28 | 157.400 | 162.000 |
| 84 | 157.225 | 161.825 |
| 85 | 157.275 | 161.875 |
| 86 | 157.325 | 161.925 |
| 87 | 157.375 | 161.975 |

VHF-FM Coast Stations are found throughout the United States. Write to the FCC, Washington, D.C., for a directory of their locations. If a particular area is not currently covered by VHF-FM service, boats can use the land mobile radiotelephone service to make telephone calls.

Coastal Harbor Service
The Coastal Harbor Service can be used over a greater distance than the VHF-FM Service, but its range is quite variable — from under 100 miles to over 1000 depending upon time and skip conditions. By January 1, 1977, this service will be completely converted from double to single sideband. Consequently, many of the former marine frequencies already on SSB between 4 and 22 MHz will be changed to accommodate the new ranges making it necessary for some boat owners to purchase different crystals. Check with the nearest FCC office to find out if this conversion affects your set. The FCC can also provide you with a directory of the locations of Coastal Harbor Service stations.

High Seas Service
This is a long-range service covering most of the world. In the USA it is operated by A T & T from stations in New York, Florida, and California, and uses a wide range of frequencies between 4 and 22 MHz. Only large yachts would be equipped to use this service. For further information contact the nearest Bell Telephone office.

**Making and receiving calls through a Public Coast Station**
To make a call through a Public Coast Station, first listen to find out if the station's channel is in use. If it is, try

switching to one of the station's other working channels. When you locate an available frequency, switch to transmit and say the name of the coast station you are calling. Then say THIS IS followed by your call sign. If there is no answer, wait a while and try again. When the coast station replies, proceed by saying THIS IS followed again by your call sign and this time also by the name of your boat and your boat's telephone number, if any. Then tell the operator the number you are calling. Say: CALLING followed by the number you want to reach. At the end of your conversation, sign off by giving your call sign and your boat's name, ending with the word OUT.

Before a coast station operator will put through your call, you must also provide the name and address to which the bill should be sent. You can save a great deal of time when making calls by officially registering this information in advance with the coast station in your area. There is no registration fee. If your local station is part of the Bell System, you can register or obtain additional information by calling the nearest Bell Telephone office. For stations outside the Bell System, call the station itself.

When receiving a call through a public coast station, a boat's receiver must be set on the correct frequency. A VHF-FM coast station in the Bell System will call on a working channel when it has selective signalling; otherwise, it will use the distress/calling frequency 156.8 (Channel 16). A Coastal Harbor station will normally call on its working frequency in the 2 MHz band, although if the land based caller specifies, the station will use the 2182 kHz distress/calling frequency instead.

*4. Communication with the Coast Guard*
The US Coast Guard primarily uses VHF-FM communications and in most areas maintains a continuous listening watch on 156.8 MHz (Channel 16). In addition, all major Coast Guard units performing Search and Rescue (SAR) operations are equipped to communicate on 2182 kHz.

After contacting a Coast Guard unit on a distress/ calling frequency (156.8 MHz or 2182 kHz), you will be shifted to a working frequency—156.6 MHz (Channel 12) or 2670 kHz if you are in contact with a Coast Guard station, and 156.3 (Channel 6) or 2638, 2670, or 2738 kHz if you are in contact with a Coast Guard vessel.

The Coast Guard does not use the 27 MHz (*Citizens' Band,* CB) channels and does not intend to install CB radios in Coast Guard stations or vessels. It plans to expand VHF-FM coverage rather than appropriate funds for introducing CB. Therefore, use CB only for private, short-range (15 miles) communication and not for distress signals.

*5. National Weather Service Broadcasts*
Weather forecasts for coastal areas are issued every six hours by the National Weather Service. They are transmitted at intervals of four to six minutes and are updated regularly. The VHF-FM weather broadcast receiving frequencies are 162.400 and 162.550 MHz. You should be able to receive one of these channels in most areas of the United States. The information provided includes such things as wind, sea, and visibility conditions, radar summaries, and general weather predictions. Severe weather warnings often interrupt regular transmissions.

## Loran 'C'

In many races in the United States Loran 'C', a low frequency hyperbolic radio aid to navigation, is permitted. Signals are transmitted from stations located in coastal areas, mostly in the northern hemisphere. Simply put, the difference in arrival time of two signals is measured to give lines of position (LOP's). The LOP's are then plotted on a special chart to obtain a fix and the ship's position. US Coast Guard handbook number 462 gives further information. Apply to the nearest C.G. station for a copy and for a list of Loran 'C' charts.

## Official and unofficial US publications on radiotelephone stations

The rules governing the installation and use of radiotelephone stations in the US are contained in volume IV of the FCC's Rules and Regulations, Part 83: 'Stations on Shipboard in the Maritime Services'. All ship radiotelephone stations must have a copy. Since the rules are continually amended, the information you read here may already be somewhat out of date, so always consult the complete text of the latest Rules. You can buy a copy of volume IV and a subscription to any new amendments from the Superintendent of Documents, US Government Printing Office, Washington, D.C. 20401.

A useful unofficial publication, 'Marine Radio Telephony', is put out by the Radio Technical Commission for Marine Services, P.O. Box 19087, Washington, D.C. 20036. It is a fifty-page booklet describing many aspects of how to operate marine radiotelephone equipment correctly.

# 14. First aid

by Dr Jonathan Rogers MA MB BChir

The skipper should look after the health of his crew in the following manner:

1. Be aware of individual members' health problems and physical limitations, history of heart disease, epilepsy, diabetes and if taking tablets.
2. Be aware of effect of environment on crew, heat and sunburn, cold and exposure; remind crew to dress properly and give them opportunity to do so. Try to avoid unnecessary wet clothing by foresight and organization.
3. Facilitate good ventilation below for off watch crew.
4. Keep the crew drinking. Fluid requirement at sea is very high.
5. Food is best thought about before a voyage and the skipper should organize regular small meals.
6. Be aware of the problems of regular relief of bowel and bladder, and make this easy for male and female members of the crew. This applies even to a day race or passage.

**Approach in event of illness or injury**
Someone, usually the skipper, must take responsibility to help, and *must* go through the following procedure if unnecessary mistakes are to be avoided. Get the patient to one side with just a modicum of privacy.

1. Take a 'history'
    (a) What is the complaint?

(b) Previous similar trouble and treatment
(c) Previous serious illness
(d) Does anything make it better or worse—position, food, movement.
(e) General questions which *MUST* be asked:
    1. Are waterworks OK? No pain or frequency?
    2. Bowel: Constipation or diarrhoea?
    3. Menstrual periods normal?

2. *Examination* This *must* be done, albeit in a very simple form. Look where pain is or at rash etc.

Take the patient's temperature and pulse. Look for deformity of the body—compare one side to the other to highlight deformity. Press gently for tenderness. If relevant expose the abdomen and feel for tenderness. Judge whether abdomen is soft or iron hard, but must relax the patient.

3. *Treatment* Nursing is the most important thing.

Reassurance and calm, ventilation, temperature control, fluids, relief of pain, specific treatment if you can.

This must be limited by competence of 'the medic'. Special knowledge or training will make you more prepared to give injections etc., and you may want to add to the simple system laid out below.

Before you start ALWAYS ask 'have you ever been upset by drugs before?' e.g. Penicillin, or Aspirin, etc.

## Medical Kit
*Equipment*
2 thermometers
1 pair surgical scissors
2 artery clips (one can be used as a needle holder)
1 toothed forceps
1 splinter forceps
black silk suture material and needle
3 5 ml sterile syringes (disposable)
6 23 g hypodermic needles (disposable)
1 bottle Lignocaine 1% local anaesthetic

*Dressings*
1 box Elastoplasts
1 roll cotton wool
12 sterile gauze dressings
4 3" crepe bandages
2 rolls 1" micropore paper tape plaster

## Drugs
1. *Antibiotics*
60 Penicillin 250 mg tablets
one—4 times a day for adults
one half—4 times a day for child under 8 yrs. Safe in pregnancy.
40 Ampicillin 250 mg capsules (wide spectrum antibiotics for severe infection). Safe in pregnancy
one—4 times a day for adults
one half—contents of one capsule—4 times a day for a child under 8 yrs
40 Tetracycline 250 mg tablets. Not safe in pregnancy.
Use if sensitive to Penicillin and in ordinary chest infections; one—4 times a day for adults; one half—4 times a day for a child

2. *Fever reducing drugs*
100 Soluble Aspirin 600 mg tablets (Disprin)
Two—4 hourly for adults
one—6 hourly for 5–8 year old child
one half—4 hourly for 2–5 year old child
100 Paracetamol 500 mg tablets. Used as for soluble Aspirin. Preferable if there is a history of sensitivity to Aspirin, or if the 'tummy is upset'.

3. *Control of Bowels*
1. 60 Senokot tablets. One or two tablets at night. Remember, constipation at sea is the result of dehydration and the physical difficulty of opening the bowels. Make crew drink fluids and be sure people can go.
2. 100 Chalk and Opium BPC Tablets. For diarrhoea 3 tablets every 4 hours until diarrhoea stops for adults.
2 tablets 6 hourly for children under 8 years
Do not use for children under 4 years

4. *Allergies, rashes and infections*
30 piriton tablets (Chlorpheniramine) 4 mg
1 tablet 3 times a day for adults down to 12 year olds
1 tablet a day for 5 to 12 year olds
150 ml Calamine lotion
15 g Neobacrin antibiotic ointment
15 g Cicatrin antibacterial powder for moist infected grazes etc.
15 g Tinaderm ointment for foot and groin rashes
15 g Hydrocortisone ointment 1% for allergic rashes and anal irritations
2 tubes 4 g Chloromycetin 1% eye ointment—Four times a day. Throw away after course of treatment.

5. *Nausea and Vomiting*
Stemetil 5 mg tablets (Prochlorpera-
zine) —four hourly if required
Use Phenergan Syrup for children (see
sedatives)
Stemetil suppositories—one 6 hourly
for adults if vomiting has started.

6. *Pain relief*
Soluble Aspirin and Paracetamol are
good pain relievers (see fever control)
20 Pethidine Tablets 50 mg—only for
severe pain
Adults—two tablets at once then one
4 hourly only if required.
Remember may cause nausea: if this
occurs give Stemetil tablet with each
dose
Children—5–12 years—one half tablet
to control pain then use Aspirin or
Paracetamol.

7. *Phenergan Syrup*
5–15 mls as a single dose to help a child
sleep or in preparation for a voyage if
the child suffers from sea sickness.

## Illness and treatment

1. *Fever*
The medic should always establish
whether fever exists or not by taking the
temperature. Flushing and sweating may
occur through poor ventilation but temperature is normal. Confirmation of a
serious illness can be made by finding a
high temperature in someone who appears
normal. If the body temperature is raised
the patient must have the minimum of
clothing so that heat may be lost into the
atmosphere. Do not let the patient,
especially a child, cover himself up.
Leaving clothes on a young child who
has a fever can result in febrile fits. The
patient may complain of cold, but if the
temperature is raised he must not wrap
himself up.

## Causes—infections

1. *Local* Presence of redness, pain and
tender lymph glands in the general area
of the pain suggest infection. Rest the
infected part if possible, splint a hand or
use a sling, drain any visible pus using a
sterile disposable needle. Use Penicillin.

2. *General* Cough, severe sore throats etc.
Control temperature using good ventilation, fluids by mouth and Penicillin. If
the fever is high use Ampicillin. Bowel
infections producing diarrhoea—starve
the patient of all solids—give frequent
small drinks, chalk and opium tablets.
Urinary infections producing painful frequent passing of water—ampicillin and
high fluid intake.

3. *Sunstroke* Excessive exposure to the
sun can produce fever often associated
with fairly severe sunburn. Control fever
with Disprin and good ventilation and
give ample fluids.

2. *Abdominal pain*
(a) Take a careful *history* of previous
abdominal pain and operations. Has he
had his appendix removed; does he suffer
from ulcers? Ask about bodily functions,
bowels, urine and periods. This is often
the cause of abdominal pain in young girls
and women 12 years and upwards. Usually
24 hours before period starts, but also
ovulation pain 14 days after first day of
previous period. Ask about the site of pain,
and what makes it better. Milk etc. improves indigestion; or what makes it
worse, pressure, exercise.

(b) You must *examine* the patient. Lie him/her down and allow to relax. Put your hand on the abdomen and if the abdomen feels soft in spite of areas of tenderness you are probably safe for the moment, although you should re-examine frequently. If there is iron hard resistance to gentle pressure, plus the presence of fever, you must seek help as soon as possible. If there is bound to be delay, then start the patient on Ampicillin and continue it for seven days.

(c) Immediate problems. Several conditions can cause very severe abdominal pain often associated with vomiting. Kidney stones cause severe left or right sided pain which doubles the patient up. There is usually some association with frequency of, or pain on, passing water. Give fluids and control pain with Pethidine. Bowel colic is often part of a bowel infection with diarrhoea. General abdominal pain often precedes the opening of the bowels. The presence of marked diarrhoea makes serious intra abdominal disease more unlikely.

### 3. Chest pain

(a) A coronary must be considered. Heart pain is usually central, but may spread out into the neck and down the left arm. *It can be made worse by exercise* and is associated with shortness of breath. Treatment is by resting the patient, providing good ventilation, and control of the pain with Pethidine.

(b) Other causes. Pleurisy can cause severe pain which is made worse by breathing deeply. It is always associated with a fever. Give Ampicillin and control the pain.

Strain or bruising of chest muscles is also made worse by deep breathing. There is tenderness when the chest is pressed, but no fever.

### 4. Collapse

Immediately establish an airway. Remove false teeth. If unconscious lie flat with head turned to one side and lift the patient's chin to facilitate breathing. *A crewman must be delegated to watch* that the patient's breathing is not obstructed.

Causes may be due to a very large *coronary,* in which case the pulse is weak and patient cold. A *stroke,* when movement of one side of the body is absent and the face distorted. *Epilepsy* when loss of consciousness is associated with violent jerking movements. (These will pass and the patient must be prevented from hurting himself and his airway must be maintained).

The only treatment possible is that of careful nursing which guarantees the patient can breathe, and that blood flows to the brain by lying patient flat.

If consciousness returns a history should be taken and sites of pain etc. examined. If respiration stops, resuscitation should be attempted.

*Resuscitation* (for collapse; for drowning see page 115)

Lie the patient on a hard surface face up, breathe 4 or 5 times into the patient's mouth while pinching his nose, observing that his chest inflates as proof of air going into his lungs. Make sure that he can vomit or drain fluid by placing him in a head down position, if possible. A child can be laid head down across your knee. Should the heart stop, 4 or 5 firm pushes to the centre of the chest may establish it again.

113

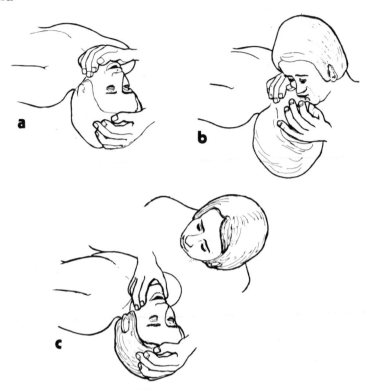

Fig 25. Mouth to mouth resuscitation. (a) Head should be tilted fully backwards. (b) Breathe into mouth while pinching nose. (c) Watch for chest movement, while taking deep breath for next exhalation. Start with four or five quick breaths, then slow down to about ten per minute.

## Visible or external accidents

1. *Body injury*
(a) The skipper must *gain control* of the situation. He must be cool, calm and firmly give directions to the crew. He must *control obvious haemorrhage immediately by pressure with the hand.*

Then remove patient to safety where further injury will not occur and make him comfortable. Pethidine may need to be given early so that an examination may be undertaken without distress.
(b) *Examination.* Look over the whole body. Major fractures may disguise other serious injuries. Splint any limb that

appears to be damaged using cotton wool and crepe bandages round a sail batten.

(c) Treatment. Control haemorrhage using local pressure only. Do not use torniquets. Deep lacerations must be sutured as soon as possible. Any delay makes the procedure more difficult. Inject lignocaine into both sides of the cut. Use artery clip to control arterial bleeding. After 3 or 4 minutes during which the cut is cleaned by firm pressure with a pad of dressings, the stitches are put in. Use another artery clip to hold the needle and the toothed forceps to hold the skin. Put single stitches entering the skin at least $\frac{1}{4}''$ from the edge of the cut. Tie the suture so that the skin is drawn together. Apply a clean dressing. Salt water must be kept away from the cut until the stitches are removed (in seven days). Minor lacerations may be closed using strips of micropore paper tape.

## 2. *Head injuries*
Cover the wound—suturing may be necessary. Do not remove any deeply embedded foreign body or bone splinter. Put patient at rest, keep a record of the pulse and general condition every $\frac{1}{4}$ hour. Should the level of consciousness deteriorate help must be sought. If the pulse remains steady and the patient is easily roused there is probably no serious damage. Only use Pethidine if absolutely necessary as it may make assessment of level of consciousness difficult.

## 3. *Drowning and exposure* (Fig 25)
*Water must be removed* from the lungs rapidly. A flat or head down posture may be enough to do this. The *airway must be clear*—remove false teeth and lift chin. If there is no respiratory movement, *breathe into the mouth and pinch the nose.* Firm pressure on the chest may facilitate the drainage of the water.

*Exposure* will produce shock and a low temperature. Strip the patient naked and then wrap him/her in thin dry garment and rest him in a warm environment.

*If you wrap a cold person up you will keep the cold in.* The source of heat must be inside any 'insulating' blankets or clothes. If the cabin cannot be heated the body warmth of a crew member lying with the patient may be needed.

## 4. *Eye injuries*
Painful red eyes should be carefully examined for the presence of a foreign body. Remove this if possible, and use Chloromycetin eye ointment four times a day. Put a pad over the eye.

## 5. *Burns*
Immediately remove burnt or hot clothing. Cool the burnt area of skin with cold water for up to half an hour. Control the pain if necessary with Pethidine. Cover the area with clean dressing. Do not use ointments unless infection appears later on and then Cicatrin powder is best. Blisters full of fluid should be allowed to drain naturally themselves. Give the patient a lot of fluid to drink.

## 6. *Seasickness*
The skipper must make every effort to prevent this miserable condition. He can do this in several ways. The 'Friday night' rush from the pub to the boat is a very common cause, and really the resulting misery is just not worth it. The crew should be rested and should start the voyage on half empty stomachs. The skipper should make it clear that he is sympathetic about seasickness. Nervous

## first aid

tension, fatigue, poor ventilation, diesel fumes etc. make seasickness more likely. Cold and overheating are also a common cause. The skipper must watch his crew and ask them to go and put on more clothes or take clothes off. He should look for early signs, such as lack of colour, lassitude, yawning, and talk to them giving them jobs to do.

When vomiting starts he must look after them or delegate someone else to do so. A person vomiting is in great danger of falling overboard. Hang on to him. The treatment is rest, and a Stemetil tablet every 4 hours with small frequent drinks of fluid. If the vomiting persists the patient should be put below and a Stemetil suppository given.

A friendly understanding approach to seasickness can cure a person of this affliction so that he never again fears it when sailing offshore.

*In the United States, the Coast Guard puts out a useful booklet on first aid (publication AUX-206), which is free. To get one, write or call the Commander of the Coast Guard District nearest you. Local chapters of the American Red Cross also offer courses in various aspects of first aid and boating safety.*

# 15. Measures and metric equivalents

A variety of units for measuring all sorts of things is used at sea—cables, metres, millibars, decimal feet, degrees Farenheit and minutes of arc! Whatever attempts at uniformity there may be, the fact is that metric, English and American units are all in use. This section is mainly concerned with quick reference equivalents and some explanations.

**Typical boat lengths and rating figure equivalents**

| Metres | Feet/decimals | Feet/inches |
|---|---|---|
| 5·5 | 18·0 | 18–0 |
| 6 | 19·7 | 19–8 |
| 6·1 | 20·0 | 20–0 |
| 6·6 | 21·7 | 21–8 |
| 7·5 | 24·5 | 24–6 |
| 7·9 | 26·0 | 26–0 |
| 8·4 | 27·5 | 27–6 |
| 9·1 | 30·0 | 30–0 |
| 10 | 32·8 | 33–0 |
| 12 | 39·4 | 39–6 |
| 12·2 | 40·0 | 40–0 |
| 15·2 | 50·0 | 50–0 |

*Areas* (Sail area)
1 square metre = 10·76 square feet
1 square foot = 0·93 square metres
(for rough equivalent just move decimal point)

**Linear and area measure**

International nautical mile is 1852 metres. UK nautical mile is 6080 feet: this is 1853·18 metres (0·06 per cent greater than the international mile, so negligible difference). A minute of latitude is for practical purposes equal to one nautical mile. Actually it is shorter at the equator (6046 ft.) and longer at the poles (6108): these differences are negligible. A statute land mile is 5280 ft, so it is very different (by some 15 per cent). Knots and m.p.h. do not therefore approximate.

One cable is $\frac{1}{10}$ of a nautical mile. So it is 185 metres or just over 200 yards (202).

Both English and metric measure will continue in many aspects of international sailing for many years, so equivalents will be needed. Useful ones are:

1 inch = 35·4 mm
1 foot = 204·8 mm
1 metre = 39·4 inches
100 metres = 328 feet
1 yard = 0·914 metres

# measures

## Dimensions on charts

British Admiralty charts, issued by the British Ministry of Defence, are changing to metric notation. The main difference is that depths are in metres rather than feet and fathoms. There are also numerous revisions of symbols and presentation. The key to these is in a 32 page book called 'Chart 5011. Symbols and Abbreviations'.

A single figure sounding, e.g. 17 indicates metres but $17_4$ indicates 17 metres and four tenths of a metre. Heights are also in metres, above mean high water spring tides. m indicates metres: M indicates nautical miles usually when giving the range of a light.

Note on range given on Admiralty charts: On metric charts the range of light given is the *nominal* range. This is related to the strength of the light and an observer on a yacht at only, say, 8 ft above sea level may not be able to see if beyond a distance (*geographical* distance) dependent on the *height* of the light. Calculate this from standard tables.

## Depth

Because of charts and instruments being variously in feet, fathoms and metres, a full table of equivalents should be posted near the chart table.

| | | |
|---|---|---|
| 1 metre = | 3·281 feet = | 0·547 fathoms |
| 1 fathom = 6 feet | = 1·8 | metres |
| 2 fathoms = 12 feet | = 3·6 | metres |

## Velocity of sound in air

In still air at 15°C this may be taken as 340 metres per second. In warmer weather it will be faster (colder, slower). Allow for wind speed, if appreciable (e.g. 3% at Force 5).

## Distance with time

1 knot = 1 nautical mile per hour
1 knot = 1·15 statute miles per hour (m.p.h.)

Measured mile tables: these are in reference books for ships and give speed in knots against the time taken on trials to cover one nautical mile over a measured and marked distance.

### Passage times at yacht speeds

| Average speed | $2\frac{1}{2}$ | 4 | 5 | 6 | 8 knots |
|---|---|---|---|---|---|
| **Distance (miles)** | | | | | |
| 10 | 4 | $2\frac{1}{2}$ | 2 | $1\frac{2}{3}$ | $1\frac{1}{4}$ hours |
| 30 | 12 | $7\frac{1}{2}$ | 6 | 5 | $3\frac{3}{4}$ |
| 50 | 20 | 12 | 10 | $8\frac{1}{3}$ | 6 |
| 100 | 40 | 25 | 20 | $16\frac{2}{3}$ | $12\frac{1}{2}$ |
| 200 | 80 | 50 | 40 | $33\frac{1}{3}$ | 25 |
| 250 | 100 | $62\frac{1}{2}$ | 50 | $41\frac{2}{3}$ | $31\frac{1}{4}$ |
| 600 | 240 | 150 | 120 | 100 | 75 |

## Temperature equivalents

Fahrenheit to Centigrade: to convert, first deduct 32, then multiply by 5 and divide by 9.

Centigrade to Fahrenheit: to convert, multiply by 9, divide by 5, then add 32.

| Centigrade° | Fahrenheit° | |
|---|---|---|
| 0 | 32 | (freezing point) |
| 5 | 41 | |
| 10 | 50 | |
| 15 | 59 | |
| 20 | 68 | |
| 25 | 77 | |
| 30 | 86 | |
| 37 | 98·6 | (blood heat) |
| 100 | 212 | (boiling point) |

## Wind Speeds

| Mean speed in knots | Beaufort scale | Metres per second (used in Scandinavia) |
|---|---|---|
| 2 | 1 | 1 |
| 5 | 2 | 3 |
| 8½ | 3 | 4 |
| 13½ | 4 | 7 |
| 19 | 5 | 10 |
| 25 | 6 | 13 |
| 30 | 7 | 15 |
| 37 | 8 | 19 |
| 43 | 9 | 22 |
| 50 | 10 | 26 |

## Capacity and liquid equivalents

| | |
|---|---|
| 1 litre | = 1000 cubic centimetres |
| 1 litre | = 0·22 (UK) gallons |
| | = 0·26 (USA) gallons |
| 1 (UK) gallon | = 4·5 litres |
| 1 (USA) gallon | = 3·75 litres |
| 8 (UK) pints | = 1 (UK) gallon |
| 8 (USA) pints | = 1 (USA) gallon |

So UK and USA pints and fluid ounces remain in same proportions as their respective gallons.
Rough guide: 1 litre is about 1¾ (UK) pints and 2 (USA) pints.

## Barometric pressure

| | |
|---|---|
| 980 millibars equal | 28·94 inches |
| 990 | 29·23 |
| 1000 | 29·53 |
| 1010 | 29·82 |
| 1020 | 30·15 |
| 1030 | 30·42 |

## Weight equivalents

| | |
|---|---|
| 1 kilogramme | = 2·2 pounds (lb) |
| 1 pound | = 0·45 kilogrammes |
| 1 tonne | = 1000 kilogrammes |
| 1 ton | = 2240 pounds |
| 1 ton | = 1·02 tonnes |

# 16. Race organization

**Introduction**

The fact that every yacht in a fleet comes to the line with an IOR (or any other sort of) rating is only one aspect of the ability of a club to organize a fair race. For any one yacht, the rating certificate certainly circumscribes aspects of her conduct during a race: in other words, she cannot turn up at the start line with any more sail area, or sail area differently distributed other than is shown on the certificate. Yet the owner can, for instance, put a piece on the bottom of the rudder to improve steering without invalidating his certificate. But he must be careful — there may be some other territory in the whole organized structure of a fair race on which he has trespassed. This structure has other limits which regulate fair racing (which have little to do with rating). There are class limits (is A going to race against B at all?); crew numbers; the time allowance system in use (which may make winning nearly impossible in certain conditions); age allowance (which could be affected by some non-ratable alteration to the boat); or, bans on electronic equipment which the crew may hitherto have relied on.

The ORC has realized for some time (since 1974 to be exact when a public meeting in Marblehead, Mass. pinpointed this) that for a yacht in competition, her rating value is only a small part of the system under which she races. Such realization has not been general. (See Chapter 20.) Efforts are being made (1976 onwards) to spread this concept and for that reason the ORC appointed a 'Development Committee' to handle the framework of IOR racing in a wider way than mere consideration of the current rating rule. Chapters 16 and 17 here, are concerned with the elements in this framework. Understanding of what these non-rule aspects are attempting is essential for race organizers and competitors: otherwise there will be discontent.

One facet of rating is that unlike more general rulings in yacht racing, it is a 'personal figure' rather like one's weight or size in shirts. It has, too, been paid for with a not inconsiderable fee. It is a personal sort of figure, to be proud of or ashamed! The owner, of course, wants the best. It follows that calls for a change in the formula by which rating is found are vociferous. Such changes could frequently be dealt with more relevantly by some of the allowances and organizational techniques which now follow.

**ORC Classes**

IOR classes I to VIII (always written with roman numerals to distinguish them from other class numbering systems) have been authorized by the ORC since

1970. Whatever time allowance for ratings is in force, it can seldom be fair to compare the result of a 60 ft rater with a 20 ft rater (or for that matter a 20 footer with a 21 footer, but it is a matter of degree). So classes bring together yachts of closely similar ratings, which will be racing within about the same weather conditions, so that the time allowance system can give an acceptable result. Class winners are more significant than the overall result and some far sighted race committees have eliminated this overall result (beloved, however, with newspapers who want to know 'who won?'). Races and series which have been recently established are able to work this (e.g. the Solent Points championship, only started in 1972, has never had an overall winner, indeed different classes in the same race will frequently sail different courses), but many of long standing have an important cup for the overall winner, so he has to be found. It is not denied that it adds to the fun, so long as there are class prizes as well, but committees should not run round trying to draw deductions and alter rules because of the overall result.

Semantics come into this and should not be ignored by race committees and their press officers. Expressions like 'fleet winner' or 'fleet champion' should be avoided. 'Best corrected time' is a better statement of fact and draws no conclusions. 'BCT' is even more suitably modest. After all, the overall winner himself will celebrate as happily as ever, but for the other boats, especially those with class places, the balance is redressed. As for overall places (e.g. overall 3rd) there seems no need for these to be recorded unless there are, again, special rewards outstanding. Anyway

such awards are best transferred to class situations.

The eight ORC classes are as follows:

| Class | Limits by rating | |
|------|-----------------|------------------|
| I | 33·0 ft to 70·0 ft | 10·05 m to 21·34 m |
| II | 29·0 ft to 32·9 ft | 8·84 m to 10·02 m |
| III | 25·5 ft to 28·9 ft | 7·77 m to 8·81 m |
| IV | 23·0 ft to 25·4 ft | 7·01 m to 7·74 m |
| V | 21·0 ft to 22·9 ft | 6·40 m to 6·98 m |
| VI | 19·5 ft to 20·9 ft | 5·94 m to 6·37 m |
| VII | 17·5 ft to 19·4 ft | 5·31 m to 5·91 m |
| VIII | 16·0 ft to 17·4 ft | 4·80 m to 5·28 m |

The obvious time when such classes are not practicable is when fleets are very small and of very disparate size. Such a situation seldom prevails for long: it is more common to find a number of yachts of a certain size, than just two or three 'odd ones'. It would be best then to put them in a separate class.

One important recommendation is that when it is not possible to split a fleet into all eight classes, then the 'break points' should still be on the same numbers. For instance the JOG in England has two classes: they are Class V/VI and Class VII/VIII. Similarly the Clyde Cruising Club has two IOR classes, A and B. A is for boats of 23·0 ft rating and above and B is for 22·9 ft rating and below. The CCC could have called them Class I/II/III/IV and Class V/VI/VII/VIII but this would have been too cumbersome. The influence of level rating is felt among these grouped IOR classes. Each class except I, VI and VIII has level rating boats within it. However, in a particular sailing area there may be a prevalence of one level rating class rather than another. So for instance Class VII might be nearly all Quarter Tonners, while the other IOR classes do not have such intense racers among them and show a variety of boat. This is a further reason for keeping with the IOR classes or combinations of them.

The IOR class structure has one more effect. By having a top limit of 70 ft, it creates a maxi-class of boat racing level whose owners aim to be first home in any IOR race. Naturally, there are comparatively few of such vessels.

The other system of allocating classes (apart from an arbitrary system which merely chooses different figures) is prevalent in the United States. When the entries have been received, the fleet is divided into two, three, or more, roughly equal divisions, which are then labelled A, B, etc. or 1, 2, etc., regardless of where the European classifications fall. For example, if there are 15 boats rating 40 foot and up, while the next boat rates 33 foot, the division will be put at 35 foot to obtain fairer racing in each class. One of the reasons for the use of this system in the US is the large number of yachts that fit into what is IOR Class I. This makes it almost essential for clubs to establish their own 'classes.' A drawback, however, is the fact that an owner cannot choose the class he will be in and who his opponents will be.

In Europe on the other hand, the classes are so permanent that boats are known by terms such as 'Class IV ocean racer', though level rating class terms are more and more frequently used.

### Level rating classes

An even fairer way to smooth out the anomalies of a time allowance system is to have classes, but eliminate time allowances altogether. The club could give a race for Class IV, but say that no time allowance was to be applied. As the maximum rating in that class is 25·4 ft it is likely that the race would be won by a yacht of that rating or the highest rated boat sailing. If races were frequently run like this, boats in the class would soon be adding sail area and taking other steps to bring their ratings up to the maximum allowed. This was not the way level raters evolved, but it is a round about way of vizualizing the logic of racing without time allowance.

The level rating classes are now well established and widely known, so it is hardly necessary to point out that boats are built to the rating and rules of these classes. The classes began with the presentation of the old One Ton Cup in 1965 for races for boats of 22 ft rating under the RORC rule of the time (pre-IOR). A potted history is contained in the ORC's 'Rules for the World Championships of the Level Rating Classes'—the 'Green Book'. This booklet also contains the rules for the conduct of the events and every year has some amendments: any interested owner should have the latest version. It contains the ORC policy on the classes. It is that they 'shall be part of the structure of modern yacht racing as epitomized in the International Offshore Rule. That rule is still primarily used in conjunction with time allowance systems to enable yachts of different ratings to race together. The Council therefore sees the level rating classes as yachts to the IOR, but racing without time allowances, rather than as restricted or formula classes such as were previously recognized in yacht racing . . .'.

By this it implies that they are inshore/offshore boats which can also cruise and are not to be compared with the old metre boats. In the same theme it says that if there is a change in the rating rule which shifts rating values, it will change the level rating figures so that existing boats mostly stay in class. This, of course, was done when the One, Half and Quarter Tonners changed from RORC to IOR. (Two Ton, Three Quarter Ton etc. were added later by the ORC.)

The maximum ratings for each class are laid down in feet. (Fig 26.) When a boat is measured in metres, feet are also always given on the certificate and these are what count for level rating. To save confusion metric equivalents are never given in the rules.

| Two Ton | 32·0 ft |
| One Ton | 27·5 ft |
| Three-Quarter Ton | 24·5 ft |
| Half Ton | 21·7 ft |
| Quarter Ton | 18·0 ft |
| Mini Ton | 16·0 ft |

The type of race and the program is important for the type of boat designed and constructed and the preparations of the crew. All Ton Cup championships follow this pattern:

| Days 1, 2, 3, 4 | Inspection |
| Day 5 | Olympic race |
| Day 6 | Olympic race |
| Day 7, 8 | Shorter offshore race |
| Day 9 | Spare or rest day |
| Day 10 | Olympic race |
| Day 11, 12, 13 | Long offshore race |
| Day 14 | Prize giving |

The inshore courses are of Olympic type, unless this is impossible to set. The length of the courses are laid down.

**Length of offshore races**

| Class | Short offshore | Long offshore |
|---|---|---|
| Two Ton | 175 miles | 350 miles |
| One Ton | 160 miles | 325 miles |
| Three-Quarter Ton | 150 miles | 300 miles |
| Half Ton | 125 miles | 250 miles |
| Quarter Ton | 100 miles | 200 miles |

In order to ensure capability in varied conditions, a principle of the offshore races is that the shorter race gives one night at sea and the long race two nights at sea.

Points to note about competing in the international Ton Cup events are:
1. The national authority must send a challenge to the organizing club together with a fee at least 60 days before the first race.
2. Individual entries must be sent by a specified date which must not be earlier than 30 days before the first race. (The club stipulates the date.)
3. If there is a team event in the series, teams must be nominated 48 hours before (none of the Ton Cups themselves are for teams, but are won by a single yacht).
4. All crew must be amateur (see IYRU racing rules).
5. An international jury (see Chapter 2) is in operation.
6. Crew members to laid down numbers are nominated plus one reserve and must not be changed.

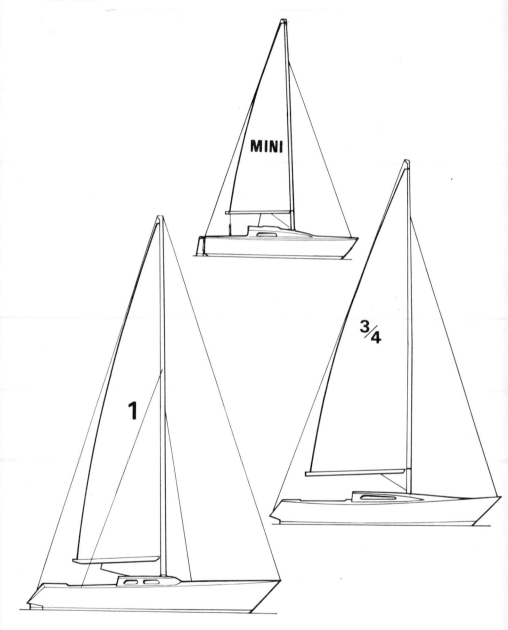

*Fig 26. The Ton Cup classes, showing
their size in an equal scale.*

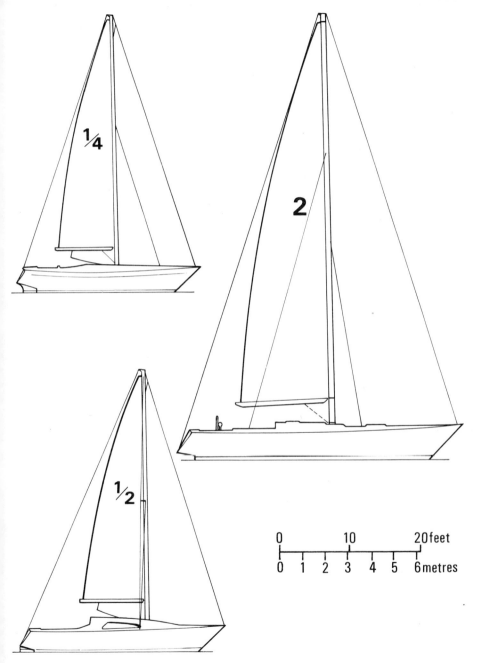

¼

2

½

| 0 | | 10 | | | 20 feet |
| 0 | 1 | 2 | 3 | 4 | 5 | 6 metres |

7. There are accommodation rules and limitations on the number of sails and on electronics.
8. Category 2 of ORC special regulations apply.
9. National prescriptions to IYRU rules do not apply.

The Green Book only applies fully to the world championships for these classes (the status of 'world championship' is useful in some countries where financial grants are allocated for events of this standing). But when national authorities and clubs run their own level rating events, they are asked to simulate the Green Book conditions as much as possible. Certainly, purely inshore series are to be discouraged and there should always be some testing offshore race in any series of standing. Boats can be sent off on an established event offshore, with others racing on time allowance, at the end of several days of inshore regattas. Time will not always permit the full international Ton Cup length of course to be used.

## Course classifications

Most IOR boats are designed to be all-purpose, but some have more emphasis on cruising than racing and some are designed for specific courses (e.g. Canada's Cup series). So a boat designed solely to win the Fastnet Race will be different in many respects to one which is intended for racing round the buoys in sheltered water every week-end. There is no official category of 'type of race', but in practice they fall into one of the following kinds (Fig 27). But everyone knows that beating for thirty miles inshore in heavy weather can be more demanding than a 200-mile glide downhill in light winds! Weather, of course, is the factor

which is not shown in these classifications and which blurs the distinctions.

## Fleet classification

New boats are built that are failures in racing due to design, equipment, organization or crewing: old boats are well sailed and win many a race. But a good new boat with a competent crew will beat a good old boat with a competent crew. A good racer with her weight in ballast and structure will again, on the 'other things being equal which they are not' principle, beat a cruising yacht with her weight in extra anchors and saloon furnishings. Such differences can be taken care of, if a club wishes to, in the following ways and the boats can then sail against each other on rating as well (IOR or any other).

Apart from the IOR classes discussed above, yachts can be divided by classes which (a) *separate certain types* or can be (b) *given allowances* which enable them to race equitably. These are the two basic systems of conducting racing with different qualities of boat. Often a combination of both methods is used. Allowances are given to individual boats, but the fleet is also divided. When the fleet is divided, all boats can start together if convenient, but separate results lists issued.

Yachts can be divided by IOR classes (or groups of classes, see above) and by the following extra divisions within classes or on an overall basis, in the case of small numbers of entries.

*Level rating prizes* The level rating boats racing among others can be singled out so that a prize is given for the best Half Tonner on elapsed time. The best boat at 21·7 ft rating or below on elapsed

*Fig 27. Classification of types of racing course used by IOR and other offshore boats.*

| Type of race | Likely occasion | Time allowance system | ORC regs category | Night sailing and offshore navigation | Race time limit |
|---|---|---|---|---|---|
| **Round the buoys** | Afternoon club race | Time on distance Time-on-time | 4 | None | Yes before dark |
| **Olympic course** | Level rating or one of a kind etc trials | Time-on-time TOD (extra distance needed for windward work) | 4 | None | Yes |
| **45–60 mile passage race (daylight)** | Weekend day event | Standard TOT or TOD | 3 | Some, possibility of being late | Possibly |
| **Overnight** | Weekend event | do. | 3 | Yes | Unlikely |
| **200–300 mile weekend race** | Weekend, or part of series | do. | 2 | Yes | No |
| **Long (600 mile) race** | Traditional course Fastnet, Sydney Hobart | do. | 2 | Yes | No |
| **Trans-Ocean** | 'One-off' event long notice (at least a year) given | Special time-on-distance e.g. $\dfrac{5143}{\sqrt{\text{Rating}}} + 3\cdot5$ secs per mile | 1 | Yes | No |

Time allowance system—USYRU tables will be used in *all* cases in U.S.

time may not be the best boat at 21·7 ft on corrected time: a boat of lower rating which is still eligible may win on corrected. The race committee may like to specify that any yacht winning a level rating prize in her class cannot take certain other prizes.

*Non-rated division* Where some yachts are IOR rated and others are not they should be in different divisions, the non-rated boats being under local time allowances or perhaps Portsmouth Yardstick. It is really better not to have an overall prize or position. It is possible by allocating the non-IOR boats local TMFs (see below) or so many seconds per mile on T-O-D. But it is not satisfactory because the arbitrary time allowances do not discipline the yachts as regards alterations, size of sails etc.

*Cruiser division* First a word on nomenclature. If there are to be separate divisions for the latest boats and the older boats, clubs should be subtle and not risk offending the owners. Organizers must choose their own terms in their own countries. There can be an 'open division' and 'cruiser division' (which we shall use here as an example). It might be better to have the fast boats in a 'special division' and the others in an 'open division'. Certainly 'fast' and 'slow' would not usually be acceptable. But this is window dressing: the important thing is how to make a dividing line.

Here is one definition: 'The Cruiser division shall comprise all yachts which qualify for an IOR Mark IIIA rating and also any other yachts which by virtue of their type are more qualified for this division than the Open division. The owners of such yachts may apply to race in the Cruiser division at the time of first entry and may be allowed to do so at the discretion of a classification sub-committee, whose decision shall be final and binding for the current series'.

An Open division might merely be defined as all yachts built since a certain date, say in the last three years; the rest of the fleet could then be left in cruisers. New genuine cruisers could then be vetted as indicated in the rule just given. In the 1976 season the RORC 'Beta' division was all yachts built before 31 December 1972 unless they had won two open prizes in the RORC races in 1975. All

later yachts were Alpha division. Prizes were given for each in all races.

A cruiser division based on equipment is another possibility. Cruisers would be limited in the number of sails of various sorts, electronic equipment, hydraulic rigging and so on. The problem here is that there would be border line cases and that such a rule involves physical inspection of yachts.

## Who starts with whom?

Because the owners in the cruiser division want the best of both worlds (and why not?), they should not be started separately. If numbers are too large for a single start on a particular start line, then the different IOR classes by rating start at intervals, cruisers and open classes in each rated class together.

If the largest boats start first they will get clear without risk of unnecessary incidents as they plough through the smaller yachts ahead, but the finish will be slightly more strung out.

## Staggered starts

For some reason these are not popular, perhaps because they prolong the work for the race committee. The smaller classes start first and the remaining ones are sent off at intervals. Depending on the race such intervals may be quarter hours, a couple of hours, half a day. The idea is that as the race progresses, the leaders will not run into quite different weather; in other words big and small boats will be in the same area (weather) in the middle part of the race. The finish will be closer, a sort of pursuit. The trouble is that it often fails to work out in practice and owners are somehow quicker to cry 'unfair' when different winds favour some boats at the start rather than at the finish.

Anyway, the policy recommended above of putting the emphasis on class prizes and cruiser etc. divisions makes the staggered start with all its extra administration unnecessary. Tidal considerations can affect starts where there are only ten or fifteen minutes between each class. The Fastnet race with six divisions (five and an Admiral's Cup class) is a classic case. With ten minutes between each class, there is an hour between first and last boats to leave. This makes an immense difference on arrival at Portland Bill, 50 miles distant, where the tide changes just about the time the boats arrive there (depending on the speed due to the wind). Naturally in such circumstances the smallest yachts are sent away first.

When there are large numbers of competitors and with this emphasis on class prizes, it is best to break down the classes into separate starts. Ten minutes is the minimum interval for ocean racing boats.

**Other organizational points**

*At what date is the yacht's rating valid for a particular race?* The answer is that any precise instructions have to be laid down by the respective club. Where there is a big entry, the club often insists that the rating is available by a certain date (say ten days before the race) and thereafter may not be changed. Otherwise it is usually satisfactory to say that the certificate must be produced before the start of the race. Where rating checks before the race are formalized, special instructions must be issued. To prevent wrangling over ratings, the club should state that the ratings on the race card issued before the race are final and valid for the race. However, a yacht owner in the same race can protest the rating so shown by lodging a protest in writing with the reasons *before* the start. (IYRU rules 19 and 68 to 73 relate). The race committee alone should be allowed to correct ratings after the start: this is a let out in case of printer's error, clerical error by the club or clerical or technical error by the measuring authority which comes to light after the start.

*Declarations* (IYRU rule 14) are in use in some countries and clubs, but not others. Point number one: if sailing abroad or in a strange area do make sure if they are required. If you do not know what a declaration is, then don't worry. It sounds as though you will never meet one in your sort of sailing. But the value of declarations for race organizers of offshore events lies in their being *qualified.* They provide a convenient way and a reminder for owners who have not fully complied with all rules, but who ask to be excused in the circumstances. The obvious case is when the engine has been started in an emergency because of man overboard or to avoid collision with a ship. The qualified declaration would explain the circumstances, why the yacht continued and how it was that no advantage was gained in the race.

*Marks unseen* A club should ensure that on its sailing instructions it is stated that, if a mark is unseen, the circumstances must be reported on the declaration. This statement would give the navigator's evidence for rounding 'by means of sounding, fog signals, radio bearings and so on'. Such circumstances arise from time to time in fog and, if this rule is not in operation, invariably result in controversy.

*Hauling out* The directions of any series of races should forbid hauling during the series. This is to avoid undue advantage to local boats and save unnecessary expense. Divers cleaning bottoms should be included in the ban. In the case of genuine damage, the owner can make a special application to the race committee.

*Electronic equipment* Since 1969 the RORC has had limitations on the use of electronic equipment. Its rule on this subject has been updated from time to time and is recommended as a basis for clubs wishing to operate such a limitation. The structure of the rule is such that it specifies what equipment *is* allowed; not the other way round, which would invite loopholes of previously unknown new equipment being introduced. It is important that certain devices are not connected together because the result can be a computer for the helmsman to 'match needles' or the navigator to read 'the best course'. The makers of this rule considered that sailing, despite all its modern aids, is a sport and these arbitrary but logical boundaries in the world of seaborne electronics preserve the sport.

The RORC rule (see also Level Rating championship rules for similar) on this subject is (1976).
ELECTRONIC AIDS, RADIO TRANS-MISSION AND RECEPTION. No electronic aid other than the following may be used in a RORC race:
(a) speedometer and log
(b) depth sounder
(c) wind speed-and-direction indicator
(d) radio receiver
(e) radio direction-finder to obtain a bearing indication either by an aural minimum method, or by a meter provided to monitor the carrier level, or both;

automatic or self-seeking radio direction-finders are not permitted.
(f) radio transmitter if used for private business or emergency purposes, or for race reporting if specified in Sailing Instructions.
(g) repeating compass provided no function is reproduced other than that of a compass card or a magnified compass card.
(h) hand-held calculators
(i) a thermometer for determining the outside water temperature with a repeater dial.

These devices may not be linked to each other in any way except that the radio receiver and direction-finder may be combined and that compass repeaters may be linked with compasses. Radar, hyperbolic navigational aids except Consol, and prearranged radio transmissions for the use of individual competitors are prohibited.

If any device other than those permitted is installed for use when not racing, such device must be provided with a clear and positive means by which it is rendered temporarily inoperable throughout a race.

# 17. Allowances for rating, age and performance

## Introduction

Time allowances are given for disparate rating, age and performance. There is frequently confusion of thought on the relationship between rating and time allowance. They are separate subjects: the allowances are flexible and easily varied; while ratings, being the result of lengthy measurement and computation, are administratively hard to change. *Rating rule changes* have effects in different directions on different boats: *time allowance system* changes have a steady 'sliding' effect across rating figures. A time allowance can also be given for the *age of the yacht,* as defined. Time allowance for *performance* can be very simple, on observations of a race or more systemized.

No internationally accepted time allowance system (TAS) exists. The ORC has had a TAS committee for some years, but this has not been able to recommend any one system. The TAS committee is not concerned with allowances for age and performance, but only in applying an allowance for use with the IOR.

## Time allowance for rating

There is of course no necessity for an international TAS. Rating under the IOR is uniform and so long as a yacht arrives for the race with a certificate, the club can apply any TAS it likes to the list of ratings. In theory it need not even decide it until after the race has started or even finished. In practice the TAS is usually settled well in advance of the race, series or even season.

No time allowance system can really be 'fair' (see Chapter 16) because even boats sailed at their theoretical best are in varied weather by reason of the distance between them. But a satisfactory TAS can be defined as one which pleases most of the competitors most of the time.

Either time-on-time (TOT) or time-on-distance (TOD) will be used in conjunction with IOR rating. From 1973 to 1974 the RORC used a combination of the two under the name of the 'Performance Factor System', (originally conceived in the ORC) but this was subsequently abandoned. Both TOD and TOT have classic but acceptable defects.

TOD: A long beat to windward or foul tide increases actual distance over that used to calculate time allowed. The smaller boat therefore does not get enough allowance. In very light weather, high ratings due to large sail area are not sufficiently penalized.

TOT: In a calm spell the boats of different sizes do not move in relation to each other, but time elapses. Therefore the

131

time on which the allowance is calculated is greater than that spent racing and the smaller boat gets too much allowance.

In November 1975 the TAS committee made—for the first time—recommendations for the use of time allowances. These were as follows.

*Time-on-time systems* should use a time multiplication factor (TMF). This TMF multiplies the elapsed time (ET) of a yacht to give corrected time (CT). The yacht with the shortest CT wins the race. The TMF is in this form.

$$TMF = \frac{k\sqrt{R}}{1 + q\sqrt{R}}$$

where R = rating; k is a constant which has no effect on results but gives a convenient figure to TMF; q is a factor which affects the time scale and is recommended to equal 0·06.

Time-on-time systems are recommended for races in *strong tidal streams and for port to port races.*

*Time-on-distance systems* should be used for conditions other than those just mentioned for TOT. The recommended general formula is:

$$\text{Seconds per mile} = p\,\frac{3600}{\sqrt{R}} + k$$

where R = rating; k is a constant which has no effect on results; p is a constant which affects the time scale; p = 0·6 or 0·66 is often used. When windward work is expected p could be higher; when downwind sailing is expected p could be lower.

### Systems in use

The longest established system in use (since 1908) is the TOD system of the United States Yacht Racing Union. In this the factors p = 0·60 and k = 0. The system is facilitated by available tables which enable allowances for all

distances to be read off direct against ratings. These tables are *Time Allowance Tables Booklet A by 10ths foot ratings* and *Time Allowance Tables Booklet B by 100ths foot ratings.* Instructions for use are given in each book, obtainable from USYRU (see Chapter 21).

A Scandinavian variant of this adds 10 per cent to the rhumb line distance. This application does not affect the formula, only the way it is applied. In the general formula if k is 401 this gives a 29 ft rating boat nil allowance, but since the application is additive/subtractive anyway, the difference from the scratch boat is taken direct from the tables.

A simple TOT system discarded by the RORC establishes a 'time correction factor (TCF) against rating by:

$$TCF = \frac{\sqrt{R} + 2\cdot6}{10}$$

The Australian TOT system uses a sixth root:

$$TCF = \sqrt[6]{R} - 0\cdot96$$

The 1976 RORC TOT system uses this formula for yachts of 23·0 ft rating and above:

$$TMF = \frac{0\cdot2424\sqrt{R}}{1 + 0\cdot0567\sqrt{R}}$$

for yachts of 22·9 ft rating and below

$$TMF = \frac{0\cdot4039\sqrt{R}}{1 + 0\cdot2337\sqrt{R}}$$

These formulae give a yacht of 29·0 ft a TMF of 1·000. Therefore she always has the same corrected time as elapsed time. Yachts bigger and smaller have larger or smaller TMF respectively: this makes CT not far from ET. There is no special merit in this.

Tables are available which list all IOR ratings with their corresponding TMFs. Rating certificates always give $\sqrt{R}$ to assist with the application of the several time allowance systems. A pocket calculator can be used to multiply TMF by ET to give CT very quickly.

From time to time exercises are carried out to determine the best TAS by checking actual results on a number of systems including the above. When these are done by class (overall results are obviously open to greater variation) the invariable picture is that the first boat and often the second and third retains its place under all systems. Only lower down the fleet do places interchange slightly.

Fig 28 is a graph which compares current TAS at fast and slow speeds, showing different speeds required from yachts of different rating.

## Time allowance for age

It is up to a designer to produce the fastest boat to the rating rule, but there is nothing an owner can do about the aging of his boat. Such things as spar sections, weight distribution and winch design do not equal the latest boats. The basic design of hull and rig may or may not be taken care of by application of IOR Mark IIIA (see page 155). If Mark IIIA is used, it is in effect a 'design allowance' and age allowance is an additional bonus. If Mark IIIA is not in use, age allowance must allow for outdated design as well.

Age allowances should be applied in the form of a percentage to TMF. Where TOD is in use they will have to be shown on the programme and applied to elapsed time, before conversion to CT.

Rules are required as to what constitutes infringement of eligibility to age allowance, e.g. alterations to hull. Re-rating alone should not invalidate it.

## Example (A) when Mark IIIA is not in

force:

'A yacht launched more than 5 years before January 1 of current racing season is entitled to an age allowance of 2 per cent to be deducted from her TMF. For yachts launched more than 10 years this allowance is increased to 10 per cent. In addition, yachts with an absolutely standard hull, the first of which was launched 6 years before January 1 of the current season, are entitled to a further deduction of 2 per cent.

Allowances under this system for 1977 season:

Yacht launched 1976 to 1971
design 2%
Yacht launched 1971 4%

The above (which is not free of loopholes) is suitable in a fleet with few new boats. Where the fleet is more modern, the following is an example (B):

'Yachts built before 2 years prior to January 1 of current season have 1 per cent deducted from TMF:'

| 4 years | 2 per cent |
| 8 years | 3 per cent |
| 13 years | 4 per cent |
| 19 years | 5 per cent |

Note on this system there is no proviso for 'standard hulls'. This is wise as such uniformity is difficult to prove and if an owner buys an old design he presumably realizes it is in some respects out-dated.

## Example (C) of age allowance where IOR Mark IIIA is in force

This is the 1976 RORC system.

'Age allowance. A deduction of 0·2 per cent of TMF per year, to be maximum of 4 per cent, using the formula given below, will be allowed to any yacht launched before 1.1.73.

0·2 (1973—year of launch) = age allowance

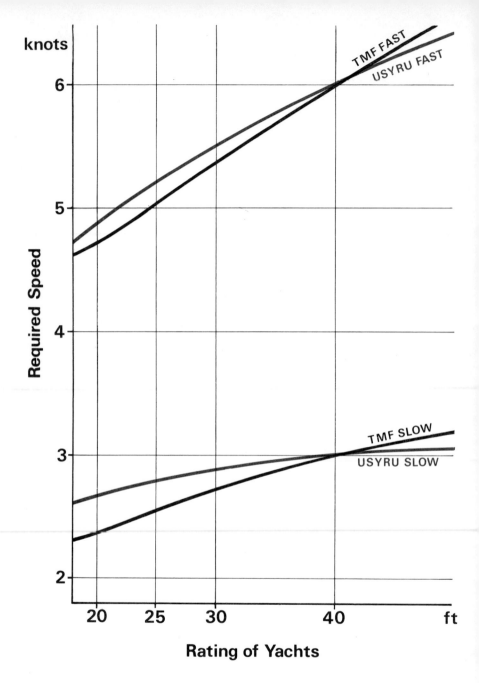

Fig 28. Under the USYRU system the smaller boats have to make better speed especially in the fast race; or to put it the other way round, in the TMF system the 40 ft rater will find it difficult to save her time in the slow race.

Speed required to equal corrected time of 40 ft yacht over 10 mile course at 3 knots (3·33 hours) at 6 knots (1·67 hours)

Unless contrary evidence is produced the year of launch will be taken as the 'year of build' on the rating certificate.

The onus for claiming and proving the right to an age allowance will be entirely on the owner. At the discretion of the committee, age allowance may not be granted if there has been, after the appropriate date, any alteration to the yacht's underwater shape. It is the responsibility of the owner to bring to the notice of the committee any such alteration'.

On this method a yacht launched 4 years before the season only gets 0·2 per cent—not much when compared with a non IIIA system.

Here is an example from a club's actual list of ratings which include IIIA and age allowance:

| Name | IOR III | IOR IIIA | AA% | TMF |
|------|---------|----------|-----|-----|
| Yacht 'A' | 26·4 | 25·4 | 1·4 | 0·9368 |
| Yacht 'B' | 24·9 | 24·1 | 0 | 0·9309 |
| Yacht 'C' | 24·0 | 23·9 | 0·4 | 0·9241 |
| Yacht 'D' | 21·6 | 21·6 | 0·2 | 0·8980 |
| Yacht 'E' | 21·7 | 21·5 | 0 | 0·8988 |
| Yacht 'F' | 21·8 | 21·2 | 0·2 | 0·8940 |

Note. Yacht 'A' gains under IIIA and AA, yacht 'B' is not old enough for AA. Yacht 'D's IIIA gives no advantage to her.

Clubs should consider whether the above is not unduly complicated and if age allowance alone (with a bigger scale but sliding steadily as in (B) above) is not more practical. On the other hand *Mark IIIA alone without any age allowance is not recommended.*

### Time allowance by performance

This works best at club level, when the same boats race regularly. Many variations exist. For instance boats may be allotted so many seconds per rule against the scratch boat by guestimate. After each race their allowance can be adjusted to bring them further up the fleet.

Adjustments are often left until after several races. The 'club handicapper' is the key man in this. For instance he may discount a particular result which has been achieved by exceptional weather or tactics. Performance systems include crew ability and simple ones cannot be transferred between club and club. They also rely on unwritten agreements in the race. For instance, if an owner modifies his rig he would inform the club handicapper who would make adjustments accordingly.

### Portsmouth Scheme

A systemized performance system is the International Portsmouth Yardstick Scheme. Under this a yacht has a *Portsmouth number* which is defined as a time over a common but unspecified distance. It means that a yacht rated at '92' will cover a given distance in 92 minutes while in the same race the yacht rated at 114 would cover the same distance in 114 minutes. As has already been seen in TAS above, this is theoretical because of differing performance in different weather. Indeed Portsmouth numbers are a kind of rating figure, but allotted by observation and not measurement. The scale of Portsmouth number comprises all whole numbers from 60 to 129 and even numbers above 129.

The essence of the Portsmouth scheme is that no yacht shall ever be without a rating. If necessary, the club handicapper will allot a provisional *Portsmouth number* to a boat which has not sailed before. Such a number is subsequently adjusted.

The reliability of a particular number is shown by means of its title as follows:

135

## allowances

*Primary yardsticks* are 'fixed' values approved by the national authority. They have become established over many races and are seldom changed. *International Primary Yardsticks are* stabilized throughout the world.

*Secondary yardsticks* are listed by the national authority but are not so well attested. They are therefore modified by

*Provisional Portsmouth Numbers* may be issued by the national authority as a guide but are not attested. The club handicapper is very likely to vary these and his assessment on the number has just as much, if not more, value.

*Langstone Tables* Given this scheme of rating numbers a club handicapper can work out any simple system for finding corrected times. However the Langstone Tables give corrected times direct from elapsed times and Portsmouth or yardstick numbers.

Even more useful, these tables give the Portsmouth number direct from an elapsed time and the corrected time of the middle yardstick in a particular race. Thus the handicapper is reading off what the Portsmouth number should have been to make the yacht place in the middle of the fleet.

*Application to cruisers* The Portsmouth scheme was originally used for centre-board racing dinghies, whose class rules ensure numbers are applicable to any boat of the class. This is not the case with cruising yachts where there is variation weight in types of engine, and in hull mouldings perhaps unknown to the club handicapper. In Britain, the RYA has established a small number of cruiser *primary yardsticks*, and a large number of cruiser *secondary yardsticks*.

Examples.

| Primary yardsticks: | English Folkboat | 120 |
| | Hunter 19 | 115 |
| | Vega 27 | 113 |
| | Westerly Centaur | 116 |
| Secondary yardsticks: | Centurion | 104 |
| | North Star 500 | 118 |
| | S & S 34 | 100 |
| | Trapper 28 Mk 1 | 107 |

There are large lists of cruiser *provisional numbers* with the limitation that the term implies.

## Action by club handicapper on arrival of a new boat

When a new boat arrives in a club fleet the handicapper can (a) estimate a number, or (b) require the yacht to sail without a number and assess one after the race or (c) base the Portsmouth number on an IOR rating if the yacht has one. (A table of approximate relationships between IOR ratings and Portsmouth numbers is available). In any case after the first race the yacht's Portsmouth number must be re-calculated on her results, giving her a first figure to enable time allowance by her performance to be made in further races.

*Base trim* The figures given above for primary yardsticks and other numbers are when the yacht is in 'base trim'. A definition of base trim is as follows:

1. Ballast as in the usual builder's specification
2. Mainsail as in the usual builder's specification
3. Genoa with 50% overlap
4. Spinnaker to approximate IOR dimensions without penalty and spinnaker boom to equal base of foretriangle.
5. Keel configuration as given in list of yardsticks and numbers

## PARTICULARS REQUIRED FROM
## RACE ENTRANTS (MONOHULLS)

Yacht's Name ................................................................................................
Owner's Name................................................................................................
Class of Yacht ................................................................................................
Hull Construction: Wood/Steel/Alloy/Glassfibre
Colour of Hull ................................................................................................
Sail No. ................................................................................................
Racing Flag ................................................................................................
L.O.A............................. L.W.L. ......................... Max. Beam...................
Max. Draft ............................ (C.B. down) ......................... Type of Rig ...............
Keel Configuration: Drop Keel (D)/Fixed Keel, central (F)/Twin Bilge Keels (2K)/Central and
　　　　　　　　　　Twin Bilge Keels (3K)...................................................
If Class Yacht is (a) Ballast Standard　　YES/NO
　　　　　　　　(b) Sail Plan Standard　　YES/NO
If NO, give details of variation from standard ..............................................

Does the Yacht carry (a) a Headsail with overlap　　YES/NO
If YES, give percentage overlap, taking fore triangle base as 100.

　　　　　　　　　　(b) a Spinnaker　　　　YES/NO
If YES, is it: approx. to I.O.R./R.O.R.C. dimensions/smaller/larger.
　　　　　　　　　　(c) an Engine　　　　　YES/NO
If YES, indicate type of installation:
　　　Outboard or detachable inboard fitted in well;
　　　Inboard with feathering or folding propeller;
　　　Inboard with fixed propeller.
Does the yacht comply in all respects with the Safety Regulations locally in force.
　　　　　　　　　　　　　　YES/NO
If NO, the yacht is not eligible to race.
Has the yacht been given a Portsmouth Number by any other race committee or organisation.
　　　　　　　　　　　　　　YES/NO
If YES please attach (or obtain and forward) Portsmouth Certificate of Number allotted.
Has the yacht an IOR Rating?　　　　　YES/NO
If YES please state:
　　IOR—Rating ........................... 　　Date ...........................

*Fig 29. A form of application for an offshore boat to enter a race under Portsmouth Yardstick.*

6. No engine fitted or carried

There are recommended adjustments to the published numbers for other than base trim. Unlike the IOR there are no precise rating changes for changes of design in this way: after all this is a performance system. Adjustment is therefore left to club handicappers. *The important point is that the club handicapper should* *adjust back from his base adjustment when submitting returns for the class to the national authority for the purpose of establishing yardsticks.*

The RYA issues suggested number variations. Examples are as follows:

Twin keel from fixed keel　　+5
Centreboard from twin keel　　−6
Fixed keel from twin keel　　−5

137

## allowances

Inboard engine with solid two blade propeller +2
Inboard engine with solid three blade propeller +4
No spinnaker +2
A convenient form for race entrants under Portsmouth yardstick which will allow the handicapper to make the necessary adjustments is shown at Fig 29.

Full particulars of the Portsmouth yardstick scheme for cruisers is contained in RYA Publication YR2.

**1977 RYA PORTSMOUTH QUESTIONNAIRE**

**Full name of Club**........................................................................................
Boat Type: **Cruiser**

| HANDICAP FLEETS | 1st | 2nd | 3rd | 4th | 5th |
|---|---|---|---|---|---|
| NUMBERS OF RACES STARTED | | | | | |
| AVERAGE NUMBER OF STARTERS | | | | | |
| RANGE OF EXISTING P.Y. NUMBERS. FROM/TO | | | | | |

**METHOD USED TO OBTAIN RECOMMENDED NUMBER**
**(Tick appropriate boxes below)**

| Time Correction | | Adjustment Made | | Adjustment Method | | Type of Water | |
|---|---|---|---|---|---|---|---|
| Langstone tables | | After every race | | By tables | | Open sea | |
| Other T.C.F. | | ..... Times per year | | By calculation | | Estuary/Harbour | |
| | | Never | | By guesswork | | Inland | |

**RETURNS**—Enter **ONLY** boats racing in **HANDICAP** fleets

| CLASS | DESCRIPTION | A* | B* | C* |
|---|---|---|---|---|
| | | | | |
| | | | | |

A* — Average number of boats in that class
B* — Number of races
C* — Your recommended Portsmouth Number

Signed ................................................................... Date ...................................................

138

# 18. The international offshore rule

## What the rule is (and is not)

Some people will say that this chapter should have been the first, before discussion of how to use the rating. In the foregoing pages the rating of any boat has been assumed and it is true that it is the basis. Yet the rating 'happens' before the boat comes to the line—usually before the entry is made. Once the race begins, the rating is one thing the owner can do nothing more about.

The IOR is a *rule of measurement and rating*. It is not a system of handicapping, not a way of giving time allowances, not an equating of performance like the Portsmouth Yardstick. Instead, a limited number of measurements, which are practical to take in a boatyard and afloat, are resolved by formulae to give a *potential* speed in the form of a linear value, which might be thought of as theoretical waterline length.

Within the rating is a means of establishing the effective sailing length of the hull and the driving power of the sail plan. There is evaluation too of speed-retarding features of the yacht—the beam and displacement of the hull which represents bulk to be cajoled through the water. Stirred in with these are such factors as the drag of the propeller, the benefits of deep draft and the quest for stability. Over the next few pages the most import-ant of the IOR formulae are detailed out and the significant measurements that have become a part of the offshore racing man's vocabularly explained.

## Now the factors

To begin at the beginning, a yacht's rating is found by the formula:

Rating = MR × CGF × EPF × MAF × SMF

where MR is the Measured Rating, CGF is the Centre of Gravity Factor, EPF is the Engine and Propeller Factor and MAF is the Movable Appendage Factor. SMF is the Spar Material Factor.

The *Measured Rating* is an assessment of the performance criteria of both hull and rig, and its formula reads:

$$MR = \frac{0.13L\sqrt{S}}{\sqrt{B \times D} + 0.25L} + 0.20\sqrt{S} + DC + FC$$

The elements of the Measured Rating Formula are:

Rated Length (L)
Rated Sail Area ($\sqrt{S}$ being the square root of the Rated Sail Area Total RSAT)
Rated Beam (B)
Rated Depth (D)
Draft Correction (DC)
Freeboard Correction (FC)

## Rated Beam

One of the most vital measurements of an IOR yacht is the Rated Beam since apart from its direct role in the Measured Rating formula it continually recurs in most of the other hull calculations. For instance its value dictates the positions of the girth stations, two of which are established at each end of the yacht, which play an essential part in the establishment of the Rated Length.

BMAX is the maximum beam of the yacht measured to exclude extraneous features such as rubbing strakes.

B is the Rated Beam, measured in the BMAX station at a point one-sixth BMAX below the sheer. Where the sectional radius of curvature at the B-measurement point is tighter than given proportions, such as in the case of a chine, B is measured at a point 0·18B below the sheerline which will be slightly nearer the waterline. (Fig 30a.)

## Rated Length

Two girth stations are located on the forebody of the yacht and two on the afterbody. (Fig 30b.) These are found by running a tape along the hull and where, at the bow, the girth is equal to 0·5B it becomes the Forward Girth Station (FGS). Similarly, the Forward Inner Girth Station (FIGS) is found by taking a girth equal to 0·75B; at the aft end the After Girth Station represents 0·75B and the After Inner Girth Station 0·875B.

The positions of these girth stations is critical to the boat's rating and it is on these stations that numerous measurements are taken which are computed to produce the Rated Length.

The order of the girth stations, from forward, is as follows:

FGS Forward Girth Station
FIGS Forward Inner Girth Station
AIGS After Inner Girth Station
AGS After Girth Station

The distance between the Forward Girth Station and the After Girth Station is the Length Between Girths (LBG). This, again, is a critical dimension as it is instrumental in providing a base for the establishment of the Rated Length.

The Rated Length formula is:

$$L = LBG - FOC - AOCC$$

where

LBG is the Length Between Girths
FOC is the Forward Overhang Component
AOCC is the After Overhang Component Corrected

The overhang components define the quality of the ends of the boat—whether and by how much they contribute to the effective sailing length. The values of both Forward and After Overhang Components are arrived at by comparing the characteristics of the inner and outer girths at respectively bow and stern. At the forward end of the yacht the essential criteria are:

FF    Freeboard at the Forward Girth Station

FFI    Freeboard at the Forward Inner Girth Station

BF    Maximum beam at the Forward Girth Station

BFI    Maximum beam at the Forward Inner Girth Station

GSDF   Girth Station Difference Forward —the distance between the inner and outer forward girth stations which defines the fullness or fineness of the forebody and the degree of overhang.

At the aft end of the yacht the essential criteria are:

FA    Freeboard at the After Girth Station

*Fig 30. IOR measurement.*

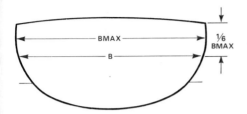

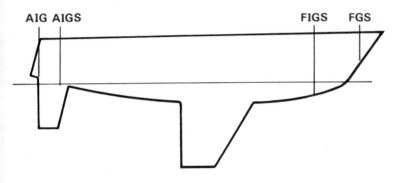

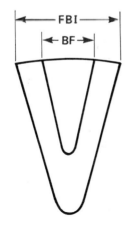

*Fig 27. (a) Finding measured beam, B.
(b) Typical position of girth stations.
(c) FGS and FIGS, the girth stations
forward.*

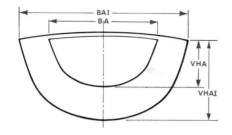

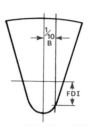

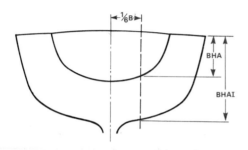

(d) Establishing the after overhang component and vertical heights (VHA and VHAI).

(e) The after girth stations using 'buttock heights' as in rule 323.

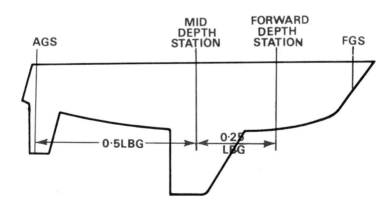

FAI  Freeboard at the After Inner Girth Station

BA  Maximum beam at the After Girth Station

BAI  Maximum beam at the After Inner Girth Station

VHA  Vertical Height at the After Girth Station measured from the sheer-line to the lowermost point of the hull

VHAI  ditto at the After Inner Girth Station

Where a boat has a particularly full stern it may not be possible to locate a girth equal to 0·75B. In this eventuality the After Girth Station will be located at the aftermost point of the sheer and the amount by which the measured girth exceeds 0·75B is recorded as

GD  Girth Difference.

This value is added to 0·875B in order to locate the After Inner Girth Station.

Where there is a hollow in the section of either of the after girth stations, as produced by a skeg or fillet, the rated slope of the profile as normally ascertained by measuring the Vertical Heights has to be established by calculated means. The procedure is to measure heights (one at each of AGS and AIGS) from a buttock line drawn 15%B from the yacht's centre-line. The difference between these buttock heights

BHA  Buttock Height Aft

BHAI  Buttock Height Aft Inner

is added to VHA to produce VHAI. When it is the After Girth Station that falls on a concavity the VHA will be found by calculating a projection through the fillet or skeg to ascertain the effective hull depth of the station.

Because of the complexity of the After Overhang Component rules and conditions this has become a busy area of exploration for designers. Indeed the success of many yachts is founded on their architects' careful appraisal of the after overhang, in particular the ability to achieve a suitable compromise between rating advantage and speed through the water. Look out therefore for changes in this part of the rule, from time to time.

**Rated Depth**

D  is the Rated Depth of a yacht, a linear dimension which equates approximately with a yacht's displacement. It is produced from immersed-depth measurements at four critical points, one in the forebody and three in the same station, roughly amidships.

FDI  is the Forward Depth Immersed, measured 0·1B from the centre-line at the Forward Depth Station which is in turn located 0·25LBG abaft the Forward Girth Station.

CMDI  is the Centre Mid Depth Immersed, measured 0·125B from the centre-line at the Mid Depth Station which is located 0·5LBG abaft FGS.

MDI  is the Mid Depth Immersed, measured 0·25B from the centre-line at the Mid Depth Station.

OMDI  is the Outer Mid Depth Immersed, measured 0·375B from the centre-line at the Mid Depth Station. This position will usually be near the intersection of the topside with the water.

MDIA  is the Mid Depth Immersed Adjusted, a linear value computed from the three midship depths. This approximates the size of the immersed midship station and fulfills a major role in the Rated Depth formula.

143

# rating rule

BWL is the yacht's Waterline Beam, measured on the maximum beam station which will not necessarily be the same as the Mid Depth Station. The relationship between the waterline beam, the rated beam and the maximum beam reflects the shape of the section and can be indicative of the sail carrying power of a yacht and of its light weather potential. BWL is computed in the MDIA formula and the Centre of Gravity Factor calculations.

**Draft Correction**

DC is the Draft Correction, a value representing the difference between a yacht's actual draft and a base draft which is established as a proportion of the Rated Length. When DC is positive the draft will be greater than the base draft and will therefore increase the rating. When DC is negative the actual draft will be shallower than the base draft and the differential will proportionately reduce the rating, although by a lesser scale than the corresponding penalty for deeper draft.

**Freeboard Correction**

FC is the Freeboard Correction and its role and application is somewhat similar to that of the Draft Correction. A base freeboard is calculated and the actual freeboard is related to this to produce the Freeboard Correction.

**Rated Sail Area**

RSAT is the Rated Sail Area Total, produced by the addition

$$RSAF + RSAM + SATC$$

$\sqrt{S}$ is the square root of RSAT, reduced to a linear measurement so that it can be computed directly in the MR formula.

RSAF is the Rated Sail Area Foretriangle

RSAM is the Rated Sail Area Mainsail

SATC is the Sail Area Total Correction, a value attached to the area differential between RSAM and RSAF. It progressively taxes the amount by which RSAF exceeds RSAM in such a manner that is intended to prevent headsails from becoming disproportionately greater than mainsails.

I is the height of the foretriangle, measured from the intersection of the forestay and the top of the mast to deck level.

J is the base of the foretriangle, measured from the forward face of the mast to the foremost stay.

P is the length of the mainsail hoist, measured between two black bands.

E is the length of the mainsail foot, measured from the aft face of the mast to a black band on the boom.

LP is the Longest Perpendicular. This defines the maximum headsail overlap and will usually be 1·5J. There is no benefit in having it smaller than this but it may be larger if the designer considers the increase in rating worthwhile. When one talks of 150% or 160% headsails one is referring to the amount by which LP exceeds J.

SPL is the Spinnaker Pole Length which is usually of the same dimension as J. There is no

144

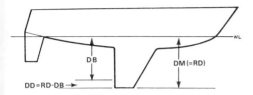

(f) Draft correction (DC) formula. DM is measured and on a fixed keel boat is RD (additional formulae for centreboarders) DB is found by $DB = 0.146L + 2$ ft. DD, (draft difference) is $RD - DB$. If it is positive $DC = 0.07L\left(\dfrac{RD}{DB}\right) - 1.0$

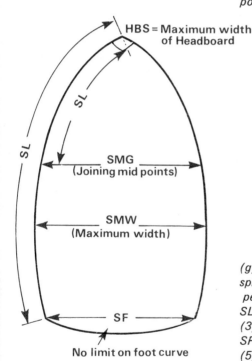

HBS = Maximum width of Headboard

SL

SL

SL

SMG (Joining mid points)

SMW (Maximum width)

SF

No limit on foot curve

(g) Terms used in measurement of spinnakers. In order to be rated without penalty, there must be (1) no battens(2) SL must not exceed $LL = 0.95\sqrt{I^2 + JC^2}$ (3) SMW must not exceed $1.8J$ or $1.8$ SPL (4) HBS must not exceed $0.05JC$ (5) No adjustable leech lines are allowed.

Rated spinnaker area, $SPIN = 1.01$ $JC \times 5L$ (or LL if greater). The spinnaker can influence the entire sail area rating because $\sqrt{S}$ is taken as SPIN, if SPIN is greater than RSAT (total rated sail area).

advantage derived from having SPL smaller than J but the rating does increase as SPL becomes larger than J.

SMW is the Spinnaker Maximum Width which is usually taken as 1.8J. Again this may be larger but only at the cost of a higher rating.

JC, IC are I and J Corrected to include 'penalties' incurred by such things as oversize SPL, SMW and SPH (Spinnaker Pole Height).

PC, EC are P and E Corrected to include batten penalties, etc.

Min.Main is the Minimum Mainsail area, computed as a proportion of I squared. This is included to protect the mainsail from extinction.

Leaving the Measured Rating formula now the other ingredients of the Rating formula have yet to be discussed, these being the CGF, EPF and MAF.

**The Centre of Gravity Factor**

In order to assess stability each IOR yacht has to undergo an inclination test whereby known weights are suspended at known distances from the yacht's centreline, usually from the end of the spinnaker pole. The angle of heel is measured for two different weights, first on one side and then on the other. Each reading is corrected to give the righting moment at one degree of heel and the figures are then averaged out to produce

RM Righting Moment.

This is subsequently related to the yacht's Rated Length and Waterline Beam and the non-dimensional product is the

TR Tenderness Ratio

which is finally computed in the CGF formula.

In order to prohibit undesirable trends a minimum value of CGF has been established as 0·9680. Generally speaking the broad, light displacement yacht of low initial stability will incline considerably better than a Metre-boat type which relies almost entirely on her lead keel for stability. Most CGF values vary from the minimum to about 0·985, although CGF values of over 1.000 are not unheard of, undesirable though they may be from a rating point of view.

**Engine and Propeller Factor**

The EPF has two vital components—

EMF Engine Moment Factor

DF Drag Factor.

The Engine Moment Factor is quite simply the product of the weight of the engine multiplied by its distance, either forward or aft, from the mid depth station. A yacht with its engine mounted in the ends will rate better than a yacht with the same engine installed amidships because it will cause the yacht to have a less easy motion.

The Drag Factor compensates for the hydrodynamic resistance produced by the propeller, strut and shaft. Needless to say the larger the propeller—subject to a maximum limit—the more beneficial the Drag Factor.

Three categories of propeller are rated by the rule—folding, feathering and solid. Only two-bladed propellers are catered for and there is no supplementary benefit for three-bladed screws. Because of the greater drag of solid propellers these naturally assume greater allowance whilst the folding propeller, which presents the least drag, is allowed the least benefit.

There are two main types of propeller installation—In Aperture and Out of Aperture. The former is less favoured now as split keel and rudder configurations are the norm; however, some boats with skeg rudders have an aperture in between the skeg and the rudder blade. Two sub-categories are listed in the rule— In Aperture Full Size and In Aperture Small —the qualifications for the one category or the other depend on the relationship between the size of the propeller and the size of the aperture.

Two sub-categories also exist for the Out of Aperture installation—Out of Aperture Exposed Shaft and Out of Aperture Other. The Exposed Shaft installation is the most common and is characterized by an exposed shaft length of at least one and a half times the propeller diameter, also by a strut of prescribed tolerances.

The rating allowance differential for the various propeller types and installation types is given as Propeller Factor (PF), as follows:

| Installation Type | Propeller Type Folding | Feathering | Solid |
|---|---|---|---|
| In Aperture—Full Size | 0·95 | 0·95 | 1·05 |
| In Aperture—Small | 0·475 | 0·475 | 0·525 |
| Out of Aperture—Exposed Shaft | 0·85 | 1·05 | 2·05 |
| Out of Aperture—Other | 0·35 | 0·55 | 1·05 |
| Strut drive | 0·60 | 0·75 | 1·33 |

As in the case of the Centre of Gravity Factor, the Engine and Propeller Factor has a minimum value which is intended to prevent the development of unusual and costly installations for the purpose of rating reduction. This minimum value is 0·9600. It is a further requirement that each installation can be proved to be capable of driving the boat at a speed equal to the square root of its rated length; again this is intended to preserve normality.

Where a boat has no engine the EPF will be taken as 1·00. In the case of a boat powered by an outboard motor the Engine Moment Factor will be taken as the EPF and the Drag Factor recorded as zero.

## Movable Appendage Factor

This is a supplementary tax on any movable appendages other than the rudder and conventional centreboard or daggerboard installations. It applies to such things as trimtabs, bilgeboards and any other appendages that have the capacity for changing their symmetry. Normally the MAF will be 1·0075 but in the case of a bilgeboarder the tax will be an addition to unity of 0·0075 for each movable appendage, and a further 0·005 if they have an angle of toe-in.

The Movable Appendage Factor is normally regarded as prohibitive, being designed to save complication and thus cost.

## The modern IOR yacht

It is not difficult to see that boats become faster for a given rating as the years pass—the designers become more experienced at designing to the rule and learn which areas will return most in terms of performance for a given degree of exploitation.

Under the IOR wetted surface area is not taxed directly and most designers have worked towards reducing this in relation to the size of boat and the sail area carried. This has been done mainly by reducing the keel area and although it is still a point of considerable argument it looks as if this development has reached its climax. The next logical development would be to design variable symmetry keels so that the lift/drag ratio could be improved for a given surface area, but because of the punitive nature of the MAF this is unlikely to happen.

Displacement in general has become lighter and hulls wider, largely to offset the reduction in Rated Depth. Despite the early intention of the rule to encourage fuller ends there is no real evidence to suggest that this has worked, although of course there are some full-ended boats around, particularly with wide sterns. However, the great proportion of competitive IOR boats are still fine in the stern, and certainly fine forward with waterplane entry angles of roughly between 35° and 45°. Most modern boats tend to be rather rectilinear in shape this is because the rule generally measures in straights and triangles and there is inadequate benefit in pursuing the full-bodied approach. At the depth stations, for instance, attempts are made to achieve maximum values at measurement points for the minimum displacement with the result that the sections are vaguely of chine configuration.

Another very discernible characteristic of modern IOR designs is the shallowness of the canoe body. The reason for this is the benefit that is conferred by the rule on forward depth. For a given displacement the designer has sought to increase the value of forward depth but in order to maintain the normal position of the longitudinal centre of buoyancy the displacement of the afterbody has had to be commensurately increased. Therefore, in order not to increase displacement, the midship sections have had to become shallower. Coupled with this reasoning is the desire to increase the effectiveness of the keel for a given draft. A shallower hull will mean a deeper keel and thus greater efficiency.

The result of this development is high prismatic coefficient (a comparative measure of displacement against the immersed midship section). Normally a high prismatic hull would be slower in light airs but by clever juggling most modern designers have got their rating parameters sorted out such that their hulls are powered by enormous rigs. Whilst they cannot fail, with all that canvas, to go well in light airs their hull shape lends to excellent performance in a blow.

With regard to sail plans the IOR looks more favourably on mainsails than fore-triangles, and on low aspect ratio against high aspect ratio. However, the incentives towards low rigs do not appear to have been adequate for, with few exceptions, rigs have become progressively taller and the emphasis shifted even further towards the foretriangle such that it became necessary to introduce a minimum area for the mainsail as a proportion of the foretriangle height.

The disadvantage of high aspect ratio from the performance point of view might have been the difficulties of cutting tall, narrow sails but sail making has progressed such that even spinnakers, with their radial concepts, are able to retain their shape remarkably well in spite of being almost tabular in shape.

Another general trend under the rule has been to increase the ratio of sail area to displacement, adding to the driving power of the boat. Sometimes this has led to control problems although it is now becoming widely felt that, sail area for sail area, modern designs are far more manageable than their ancestors.

A market characteristic of modern racing yachts that is usually beheld with regret is the way they have ceased to cater for cruising comforts. Even though the IOR, with the Centre of Gravity Factor, does more to prevent this development than previous rating rules, the competitive edge is considerably sharper and designers and owners appear to want to shed every accoutrement. It will always be a fact that a pound weight saved is a pound less water that a boat will perpetually have to push out of the way.

### Obtaining a rating certificate

Any one- or two-masted monohull may apply for an IOR rating certificate and use it providing the final rating falls between 16 ft and 70 ft. There are rating offices in most yachting areas and advances should be made to the rating office of the area where the boat will race. In some countries the owner chooses the measurer or contacts his area measurer direct. The account is also settled between the owner and the measurer. However this practice is not a satisfactory one, as the measurer tends to feel an obligation to the owner who naturally hopes for the best possible rating, whereas it should be to the rating authority that the measurer feels himself responsible. In Great Britain a measurer will then be sent to that particular boat, usually one for whom the location of the boat will be geographically most convenient. He will measure the yacht ashore first, locating the measurement stations and recording all the relevant dimensions. The second stage is to measure the yacht afloat whereby the free-boards, the waterline beam and the righting moment will be taken.

Whilst initial communication should be between the owner and the measurement authority the precise arrangements of time and place will normally be made between the owner and the measurer appointed to the task. For the shore measurement it is the owner's responsibility, as declared in the rule, to arrange that his boat be chocked up approximately level in an accessible position with the

149

weight of the keel supported from below. The owner is also expected to provide the measurer with an assistant.

## Conditions for measurement

For the flotation measurements the owner is again expected to be present or to provide an assistant, and to arrange for the boat to be moored at a suitable location for the ensuing operation. This means smooth water and no current.

There is no vital information that need be digested before measuring the hull ashore—as long as no blunders are made the hull will produce the same dimensions whether it be measured in snow or sunshine, calm or gale.

The case is slightly different for the flotation measurement because the scope for error is greater. The owner should make himself aware of his responsibilities as laid down in Part One of the rulebook, the prime one being that he should, as stated, present his boat in a location that the measurer considers suitable and to accept the fact that his yacht will be inclined only if the weather permits.

In Part Two of the rulebook a detailed synopsis is given of the required measurement trim for inclining. She will be rigged and ready to sail with a prescribed number of sails, plus the sheets and guys, stowed abaft the mast on the cabin sole. Mattresses, navigation equipment, cooking appliances and all movable gear will be in their normal positions except that movable gear normally stowed forward of the mast will be brought back behind the mast. No clothing, food or stores may be left aboard and indeed the IOR makes a point of saying that undue quantities of stores will be considered as ballast. Water and fuel tanks have to be empty if they are located forward and full if they

are located aft and as a general guide the IOR gives 65% LBG abaft the Forward Girth Station as the dividing line for this. Liferafts and dinghies must not be on board for flotation measurement and where trimming ballast is used its weight and position will have to be declared. Likewise, the position and weight of anchors and chain must be given for this information will ultimately be conveyed on the rating certificate. In addition to this long list the most obvious one of all is particularly emphasized; that is the yacht must not be so tethered to her mooring that her natural trim is affected.

Generally speaking most boats will rate better with bow-down trim. Indeed all boats with aft cockpits need to have a certain amount of inherent bow-down trim otherwise the addition of crew weight would produce a stern-down attitude which would be detrimental to performance. Nevertheless, accepting the letter of the law there is still a certain amount one can do to ensure even more advantageous trim, such as removing all loose gear from the stern of the boat— empty fuel cans, spare mooring warps, fenders and all the paraphernalia that clutters any boat. In many hull configurations the rating is highly sensitive to stern trim and for every fraction of an inch that the afterbody is lifted out of the water there is usually quite an appreciable reduction in rating.

As to the above-deck preparation the rig should not be set up too tightly, for instance the backstay should be no tighter than a tension which satisfies the measurer, similarly the shrouds. The halyard ends may be clipped to the pulpit if desired which might give a miniscule addition to the force trying to depress the yacht's head. In general, though, minutely detailed preparation will have less effect than the wide tolerances of the fairly crude method of measurement that is used. Even a measurement of freeboard can vary considerably from measurer to measurer or from day to day, depending on the amount of popple that will invariably be stirred up even in 'perfect' conditions.

Where the yacht to be measured is a series production boat the rating office may have issued standard hull figures for that design, if enough of the class have been satisfactorily measured. Nevertheless, it will still be necessary to present the boat ashore for the measurement of possible variables such as the engine and propeller installation. There will be some cost saving here, though, but the flotation measurement will be the same as for any one-off boat.

## Issue of certificate

When a rating office issues a rating certificate it will usually be a temporary one only until the rating office is satisfied with the result and until the account has been settled. However, a temporary certificate does not mean that it cannot be used for racing—indeed most new boats will race for as much as half a season on their temporary certificates. When entering races it will usually be necessary to submit the certificate as formal evidence of the yacht's rating and in level rating championships, for example, the certificates will be displayed for all to see. However, because the pressure on race officers is usually quite considerable and as displayed certificates often attract collectors it is advisable to send photocopies rather than the original certificate.

A rating certificate that may not be used for racing is an experimental certificate which is issued by some rating offices. By the letter of the rule only one rating certificate may be held at any one given time and upon each remeasurement the new certificate invalidates the previous one. What has happened, particularly as a result of intensified competition in the level rating classes, is that boats have been remeasured with the aim of perhaps reducing the rating only to produce a result that is worse than the original. In fact some owners would perpetually remeasure, hoping that one day they would come up with a 'lucky' one, spending a considerable amount of money in the process. The advantage of an experimental rating is that it does not invalidate the existing certificate so if, for instance, one were to retrim the boat with internal ballast the figures could be channelled into the rating office computer and the result be assessed. If the rating turned out as expected the owner could then certify that the boat would sail in the trim measured for the experimental certificate (and the measurer would of course want to see that this was so) and the experimental rating given the stamp of approval. However, if the experimental trim proved to have adverse effect to that required the ballast could be removed and the boat reverted to her original trim. Naturally, an extra charge is made for this experiment service, but as an insurance policy it is well worthwhile. For likely effect of changes see Fig. 31.

## Maintaining boat in certificated trim

Once the measurement procedure is completed and the rating certificate has been issued the owner is then duty-bound to maintain his yacht in its certificated state. This is not exactly the same as measurement trim. If he changes any part of the yacht or its equipment in such a manner that would alter any of the measured values he must inform the measurement authority. In Part One of the rulebook examples are given of possible changes, such as the addition of new sails, change of propeller installation, redistribution of internal ballast, structural changes to the yacht, hull modifica- by filler and fairings, etc.

By signing his IOR certificate, which is necessary to ensure its validity, he enters into other obligations which apply when racing, and he must also ensure that his crew is also familiar with the full conditions. For instance each sail has prescribed limits outside of which it may not be set, as laid out in Part Eight of the rulebook. In addition no movable gear may be shifted for any reason other than to fulfill its primary purpose, thus prohibiting the use of movable ballast. Naturally enough, shifting ballast in the form of water and fuel is also prohibited.

Some measurement authorities now issue labels which must be displayed on a bulkhead or other suitable location. These convey essential information of the yacht's measurement state—the position of the liferaft, anchor and chain, internal ballast, etc. Although this may appear to acknow- ledge the existence of underhanded practices, at least it allays the possibility of suspicion by throwing open the heart and soul of the boat.

### Competitor's certificates

Another way in which the IOR defies secrecy is the provision by which anyone might obtain, for a copying charge, a competitor's rating certificate. In fact there is a clause in the rule which specifies that every measurement authority must provide this service. The effect of this is twofold: firstly it promotes greater honesty in that the vital measure- ments of any boat are by no means classified information; secondly it allows the student of yacht design every oppor- tunity to research the reasons behind the performance differential between one boat and another.

### Limitation on the number of sails

Outside the level rating classes there used to be no limit on the number of sails carried by an IOR boat, but from April 1977 the sails on board, during any race were limited. The terms are in rule 892 and this includes details of special provisions for two masted rigs. A single masted yacht can carry a mainsail (and a spare mainsail under rule 851.2), a storm trysail (rule 851.3) and a storm jib whose dimensions are specified (see Fig 15, page 67).

Above this there are a certain number of spinnakers and jibs by rating. Under the rule 'jibs' includes all fore and after headsails such as genoas, staysails, big- boy/bloopers, reachers and drifters. The scale is as follows:

| Rating in feet | Jibs shall not number more than: | Spinnakers shall not number more than: |
|---|---|---|
| 16·0 | 3 | 1 |
| 16·1–19·4 | 5 | 3 |
| 19·5–22·9 | 6 | 3 |
| 23·0–28·9 | 6 | 4 |
| 29·0–36·0 | 7 | 5 |
| 36·1–43·0 | 8 | 5 |
| 43·1–51·9 | 9 | 6 |
| 52·0–62·0 | 10 | 6 |
| 62·1–70·0 | 11 | 6 |

*Fig 31. Table of likely changes for the rating of a yacht when various alterations are made.*

| | | | |
|---|---|---|---|
| **Use micro-balloons to build out measurement points such as B, BWL and FDI.** | Hull/ Flotation | | Will decrease rating but usually also hinder performance. There are rules about local distortions so check with measurement authority. |
| **Install lighter engine** | Flotation | EMF − /EPF + /L ± / D + | Marginal increase in rating and performance |
| **Change propeller from fixed to feathering, or from feathering to fixed, but retain the same diameter and blade width.** | Hull | PF + /EPF − | Considerable reduction in EPF and rating but commensurate increased drag. |
| **Increase propeller diameter and blade width.** | Hull | PF + EPF − | Decrease in EPF and reduced rating but higher drag. Note maximum size of propeller without further rating benefit is 0·05L. |
| **Carry outboard motor** | Flotation | EPF − | On small boats with no inboard auxiliary a small rating allowance is given for an outboard motor. Yacht must be remeasured afloat with the outboard in its normal stowage. |
| **Alter rudder** | Consult rating office | | No direct change in rating parameters unless trim is affected. |
| **Lock trim tab** | Hull | MAF − | Locking or removing a trim tab cancels MAF penalty and thus reduces the rating. |
| **Increased mainsail and reduce foretriangle by the same physical area** | Rig | P + /E + I − /J − / RSAF − /RSAM + / SATC − /RSAT − | Rating reduces. |
| **Increase aspect ratio of either mainsail or foretriangle** | Rig | (I + /J − ) (P + /E − ) RSAT + | Rating increases. |

# rating rule

| | | | |
|---|---|---|---|
| **Modifying RSAF Rig without changing I or J** | | LP ± /SPL ± and SMW ± | SPL (Spinnaker Pole Length), SMW (Spinnaker Maximum Width) and LP (Longest Perpendicular) are linked to J by the factors of 1, 1.8 and 1.5 respectively. Whilst there is no gain in having them smaller than these values they may be larger and are often used as instruments to adjust a rating to a level-rating figure. |

NB. Reduced L, DC, FC, RSAT, CGF, EPF, MAF will improve rating
　　Reduced B, D will increase rating

| | | | |
|---|---|---|---|
| **Add internal ballast forward** | Flotation | FDI + /D + /FOC − / L + /CGF ± | Increase of bow-down trim will improve Rated Depth but marginally increase Rated Length. Exaggerated bow-down trim may also incur penalty on I. CGF may be affected, usually decreased. Net effect is improvement in rating although performance and motion characteristics may deteriorate. |
| **Reduce weight of ballast keel but compensate with increased internal weight.** | Flotation | RMC − /CGF − | Trim remains the same but boat is more tender. Decrease in rating and stability. |
| **Sink boat equally fore and aft** | Flotation | FDI + /MDIA + D + / L + /CGF ± /DC + FC + /EPF − | Increase of displacement will normally reduce rating although Rated Length will proportionately increase. Best to increase sinkage forward more than aft. Propeller depth will increase, benefiting EPF, but Draft Correction and Freeboard Correction will suffer marginally. |
| **Move ballast keel forward** | Hull/ Flotation | FDI + /D + /L ± /CGF − | Increases bow-down trim which improves Rated Depth and usually also reduces CGF. Although FOC will reduce a higher flotation aft may reduce Rated Length. |
| **Increase draft with the addition of a ballast shoe.** | Hull/ Flotation | DC + /RMC + /CGF + | Increases Draft Correction and thus also rating. Will also lower centre of gravity and thus increase stability and CGF. Increases displacement for marginal rating compensation |
| **Increase weight of accommodation** | Flotation | D + /L ± /DC + /FC + / RMC − /CGF − | Increases displacement and Rated Depth. Raises centre of gravity to reduce CGF. Rating improves at the expense of sail carrying power and lightness. |

### Retrospective rating rules

A concept which, as far as is known, is completely new in the world of yacht rating rules was instituted by the ORC in November 1975. This was a retrospective rating computation to compensate for certain proportions and design features found in yachts of a few years old or older. The system was called IOR Mark IIIA.

By taking the rating certificates of yachts older than a certain date (December 1972) and applying a different formula to IOR Mark III, most yachts to which this was applied were found to have a slightly lower rating. This was essentially selective because it depended on the individual features of each boat. An 'IOR orientated' boat would not benefit so much as one with features that had more recently been found to be adversely affected in terms of speed for rating.

The whole point of Mark IIIA was that it was a rule which could not be built to. It would also be applied automatically to all eligible yachts without application from the owner. So that yachts could not be altered to get a benefit from a knowledge of Mark IIIA, there were fairly stringent rules of eligibility and limited changes as defined. Previously unmeasured yachts of unusual type were effectively prevented from taking advantage.

The use of IOR Mark IIIA was declared entirely at the option of organizing authorities, but once in use by a club its application is exactly the same as an ordinary IOR Mark III rating. The exact rulings for this system are given in IOR Mark III rule book part XI (Paragraphs 1101–1110).

# 19. More rules of measurement and rating

Several clubs and other organizations have their own rules of measurement and rating. What follows is a brief summary of each. As in the IOR, there are numerous subsidiary formulae, but here only the major formula of each rule is shown. For further information write to the relevant authority controlling the rule.

The only *international* rule outside the IOR is the IYRU rule for inshore 'metre' boats which stems directly from the International rule of 1906. It is now primarily for 12-metre yachts in which the America's Cup is sailed and is of this form:

$$\frac{L + 2d - F + \sqrt{S}}{2 \cdot 37}$$ not to exceed 12 metres.

L = length as defined in metres
d = difference of skin girth and chain girth
F = freeboard
S = sail area in square metres

There is a minimum beam, maximum height of sail plan, minimum displacement in relation to LWL, maximum height of foretriangle in relation to sail plan.

*Scandicap 73*
This is a measurement rule for keeled yachts controlled by the Scandinavian Yachting Association. Measurements are intended to be possible afloat and as far as possible taken from IOR rating certificates. The organizers reserve the right to exclude any yachts *built* to the rule.

$$\text{Rating} = (L \div B + \tfrac{2}{3}G + 0 \cdot 75 \times AR \\ \times \sqrt{(S \times SAF)}) \times PF) \div 2$$

L = Measured length = LWL + 0·03 (B + G)
B = BWL at BMAX station
G = Maximum girth below waterline
AR = Rig factor
SAF = Spinnaker factor (a lower rating can be obtained if a spinnaker is not carried).
S = Sail area
PF = Propeller factor

*MORC (Midget Ocean Racing Club)*

The rule is for boats under 30 ft racing in the USA in events organized by MORC. The rule stems directly from the old Cruising Club of America rule, which was a 'base boat' rule. Under this, corrections are added or subtracted against a rated length to give the final rating.

Rating $= 0.85(L + BMCR + DRCR + DISCR + FBCR + SACR + I) (STF) (PROP)$

 $L =$ rated length

 BMCR $=$ beam correction

 DRCR $=$ draft correction

 DISCR $=$ displacement correction (the boat is weighed)

 SACR $=$ sail area correction

 I $=$ iron ballast correction

 STF $=$ stability factor

 PROP $=$ propeller correction

*Off Soundings Club rule*

This uses data from the IOR certificate

$$\text{Rating} = \frac{L + 2 \times \sqrt{RSA} \times \text{Rig allowance}}{3} \times PROP \times UFF$$

 $L =$ Corrected length $+ 2 \times LWL - 2\,BMAX$

 RSA $=$ rated sail area

 PROP $=$ propeller allowance

 UFF $=$ under body form factor (centreboard, long keel etc)

The rig allowance is given on the basic rig such as Bermudian sloop, gaff schooner, etc.

The Storm Trysail Club has a formula also based on IOR but varying the use of the factors. It introduces LWL and defines ways of measuring this.

# 20. The IOR and its critics

## by Peter Johnson

**Credentials**

The first races under the International Offshore Rule began in 1970 when clubs in the USA adopted it at the first available opportunity (it came into force January 1, 1970). Europe followed at a slightly more gradual pace with the Royal Ocean Racing Club alone using IOR Mark II for its 1970 races while other clubs continued for that year to use the old 'RORC Rule'. IOR Mark I, incidentally, was never used for racing but was an earlier draft which was never released for use.

It is remarkable how by 1971 all rated events in Europe and, with certain exceptions, in America were using the IOR, but perhaps not surprising in view of the long lead up period during which a new rule had been promised. It may be that the rule was over-sold, especially in the United States, to a yachting public who thought that such a change would solve current rating problems for one boat or another. Yet in the same year voices were already heard about the defects and unfairness of the IOR. In September 1971 there was a meeting of the Offshore Rating Council at the St. Francis Yacht Club in San Francisco: here the complaints and dissatisfaction were for the first time brought out into the open.

At this point an explanation is in order of why this chapter has a by-line. Though analytical, there is a higher content of opinion here than in other parts of this essentially factual book. The writer has been closely connected with the IOR and the organization of international yachting for many years. It is relevant however, that he never had any part in running or promoting the old RORC rule.

With similarly minded colleagues from a number of different countries he formed 'IASORY' in the 60's, a group of clubs racing small offshore yachts, the object of which was to withstand the proliferation of level rating classes and to attempt to rationalize the numerous ideas then emerging. This organization was later absorbed into the ORC as the 'small yacht committee', a kind of pressure group to look after the application of the IOR to a specialized end of the spectrum. As a member of the RORC General Committee, the writer also found himself in a small group of men who made the decision that the RORC should abandon its own rule (one of the original reasons for its existence) and adopt the IOR. Soon after he found himself involved in bringing together the American and British safety rules in the form of ORC Special Regulations. Then he was active in the formation of a Level Rating Committee within the ORC, because up to 1972 individual yacht clubs in France had been responsible for various Ton Cup events: and yet they cried out for international cooperation and control. The system of having each Ton cup event in the country of the previous winner was abandoned, so that, instead, yachtsmen knew at least several years ahead where such events would take place and from then on they were fairly distributed around the world. From 1973 to 1976 the writer, having dropped his other duties within the ORC except that of a council member for Great Britain, became chairman of the International Technical Committee.

Having owned several boats to the RORC rule he sold the last of these in 1968 and while the new rule was emerging joined a keel boat one design class (at the same time racing on RORC boats) and then owned an IOR Mark II yacht from 1971. He changed over to an IOR Mark III boat in 1972 and so has been very conscious of the effect of rule changes upon owners. He has not had any commercial interest in design, building or the sponsorship or success of particular events.

## Early criticism

At the San Francisco meeting three kinds of criticism of the rule emerged.

1. Valid technical omissions. There were matters which could be itemized because they came to light as experience was gained in measuring boats. One of these, for instance, was a lack of measurement points in the mid section to determine MDI. Only one measurement was previously taken, but now outer and inner depth measurements were taken (OMD and CMD). (Fig. 32.) Thus a more realistic figure for the area of the immersed section at this station was obtained. (One hope expressed at the time was that this would cut out the tendency to flat bottomed hulls with thin keels because of the bonus contained from CMD. This hope was not realized and this could be a case against such rule adjustments: possibly the only result was that many yachts had to be re-measured.)

2. 'Try-ons' against the letter of the new rule. In the early days there were several attempts at dubious practices which were merely not covered in the rule as written. An example of these might be the 'water sail', a piece of cloth hung below the main boom for extra sail area. Corrections to such practices were fairly easy and merely required extra sentences inserted in the rule book.

3. The type of complaint about the rule which came more from general observation. One of the most common at this time was that the IOR 'encouraged pinched-in' ends. American yachtsmen had been accustomed to seeing sterns which were wide in plan view to get advantage from the previously used Cruising Club of America rating rule. The IOR measured the after end so that such sterns did not get the undue advantage to which they had been accustomed and therefore early boats to the IOR had trial sterns of other shapes. There was also a misunderstanding in the United States over which boats in Europe were built to the IOR and which were RORC designs, often dressed up by their promoters as IOR boats.

As a result of the discussions at San Francisco and in an attempt to satisfy what was said to be American opinion, IOR Mark II was revised and the completed revisions nominated as IOR Mark III. IOR Mark III was immediately intro-

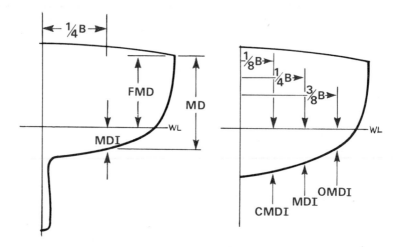

*Fig 32. The old and new system of measuring the depth. After the introduction of IOR Mark III extra measurements (CMDI and OMDI) were taken to reflect more accurately the shape of the midsection. Boats have, however, remained as flat, because this has been estimated to give better boat speed per rating.*

duced in the United States in 1972, but a year later in Europe. As re-measurements were required under IOR Mark III, considerable difficulties were experienced in the USA in trying to change over in the impending season. This did nothing to help owners' satisfaction with the rule and its administrators. In Europe there was plenty of time to measure the boats and also time to build boats to IOR Mark III ready for the 1973 season.

These events highlight the different attitudes at the time. It did seem that the American authorities were trying to beat the new designs by rushing in rule changes (which they failed to do), while the Europeans faced with a rule change

wanted to give ample time for people to adjust their boats to this change. These differing attitudes gave rise to misunderstandings especially as they applied to the same rule.

**Rule snipers**
The introduction of IOR Mark III had the reverse effect of appeasing the critics. Instead it fed their appetites, the old position being spearheaded by the appearance of the so-called cat ketch, *Cascade*. This yacht with two masts and no forward headsail is the only really successful 'freak' which has been built to the IOR. The hull was the size of a one tonner but the rating that of a half tonner: the

possibility of designing such a boat arose from deficiencies in the ruling on two masted rigs. The Council, rather unwisely, slapped on a 10% increase on the rating figure while they considered revisions in the rule. As a result they came under fire from two different directions, one set of critics saying that such arbitrary action was wrong and that the boat had been built to the rule as written, and the other critics saying that the appearance of such a boat showed that the rule was a bad one. Probably the high point (or low?) of criticism was in a widely publicized open letter to Olin J. Stephens, then chairman of the ITC, by John J. McNamara Jr. This letter, of some one thousand words, charged rule makers with gaining professional advantage from their position, using complicated techniques in an amateur sport, not knowing whether the rule was a 'handicap' or 'development' rule, and victimizing *Cascade*. McNamara said 'It has become graphically clear that IOR is a flat out development rule in an escalating spiral of hulls-of-the-month and rigs-of-the-week; it has become a paradise for committee member designers and a nirvana for sailmakers. The time is at hand for the ORC to re-think what has been wrought and to set down in clear terms a rule with a healthy and desirable philosophy'.

When the letter was mentioned at the ORC meeting at Portofino, Italy, in the spring of 1974, a resolution was passed that it should not be discussed. This was at the behest of the president of the International Yacht Racing Union (a member of the council) who said that such messages from individuals should never be accepted except when forwarded by a national authority.

## The running controversy

Although McNamara's letter was officially ignored, there were changes in the ITC composition in that year. Olin Stephens resigned and the writer took over as chairman. The other American designer, Dick Carter, who had been in the original ITC also resigned as had the Dutch designer E. G. Van de Stadt before him. The only active professional designer left on the ITC was Gary Mull from California. Yet there was now a different emphasis, with both chairman and Technical Adviser Robin Glover coming from the British ocean racing tradition. Unfortunately, a slightly different running battle now ensued between critics and rule makers. The same allegations were repeated at each ORC meeting by the principal United States delegates; the emphasis on one complaint or another has varied, but they generally included these charges:

1. Europeans are in favour of a static rule rather than a flexible rule that can be changed to meet progress in design.
2. The ITC fails to respond to design features when they appear.
3. Little is done to show the yachting public that their interests are being closely watched (by rule changes).
4. There is a lack of choice in the type of boat, especially the rig. The mast head sloop is in practice the only one possible under the rule.
5. The rule is complex and lengthy.
6. The rule fails to provide a dual purpose yacht that can race and cruise: instead only stripped out racing machines have a chance of the prize list.
7. The rule is particularly faulty in the following technical points.
   (a) Rapid 'overnight' obsolescence.
   (b) The sail areas are too large.

161

(c) The rules for measurement trim mean the accommodation is full of sails when racing. (The American critics of the time rejected a suggestion that the number of sails be limited: they only insisted that they be stowed in certain places, usually the fo'c'sle, in the yacht)

(d) Light displacement is encouraged to the extent that the yachts are undesirably light with the implication that they are therefore weak and unseaworthy.

Various United States technical committees propounded this view, but principally the technical committee of the Cruising Club of America. In 1974 it stated 'The decision of the CCA to adopt the IOR and thus to abandon its own rule affected not only its own members and its sponsored races, but also virtually all offshore yacht racing in North America. Accordingly, we believe we have some moral obligation to call for energetic and prompt response to problems of the rule. Adjustments must be made, and very soon, if the rule is to have continuing acceptance in North America'.

**Limitations of any rating rule**
It has already been mentioned that our chapter on the rule has been purposely left until the latter part of this book. The earlier chapters have considered more basic sailing requirements and this has been done because the yacht's rating is only one part of the racing effort. Expensive pleasures such as complicated electronics, masses of winches and numerous sails are nothing to do with the rule of measurement and rating. Neither are rudder failures nor broken masts. Criticisms that the rule makes for expense

or dangerous boats can be quickly dismissed. Indeed critics must decide whether they are against all rating rules or whether it is the IOR in particular that they abhor. If they are against rules of measurement and rating as such, then the IOR is, in a sense, innocent. Rating rules are not for them and they can enjoy excellent racing by other methods such as those explained in chapter 17.

But with the IOR or any other rating rule, its importance should not be over emphasized. It is notable that before a race the talk is of ratings, black bands and doubtful propeller installations. Yet after a race the talk is of winds which headed, buoys that were not identified, gear which failed at the crucial moment.

Yet after all this is acknowledged and the rule put in its rightful and quite lowly place, the critics who state that the IOR has specific faults, in comparison for instance with the old CCA or RORC rules, should be given a considered reply.

**The basic cycle**
In any rating rule there is a basic cycle of which the rule makers are conscious. Changes could be classified as being of three sorts.
1. Those that will not affect the design of yachts.
2. Those that are thought not to affect the design of yachts, but in fact do so.
3. Those that are expected to alter the design of yachts and indeed do so.

A fourth variation might be that certain effects are intended, but others are found to result and indeed possibility number 3 is normally of this type. The possibilities 2 and 3 are always there and it is a fact in the history of rating rules that an attempt to alter them to safeguard existing boats is liable to create a new design generation and therefore outdate the very boats the alteration is designed to protect. It is no good saying that alterations will be made that do not have this result: the evidence is to the contrary. One set of critics acknowledges this, but then says it would be prepared to change the rule very rapidly yet again. Yachtsmen would have to judge whether such continuous change is feasible and fair.

The fact is that the change from IOR Mark II to IOR Mark III saw a large number of new yachts which outdated the earlier IOR boats and this was surely not the aim of those who were so vociferous in asking for that major set of rule changes.

### Accusations and the facts

Year after year when the level rating races are sailed, it is quite evident that the spread of these fleets is no greater than that of a one design class. Very often the boats in the fleet look quite different in some respects, yet their ratings are evidently a very fair indication of potential speed.

Another observation that can be made is to see yachts of the same design in a mixed fleet racing under time allowance. It hardly needs saying that these boats with similar hulls and rigs are found in various positions in the fleet, very often from top to bottom, depending on the quality of skipper and crew as well as detailed equipment. The design of the boat and therefore its potential speed against rating cannot accurately be gauged in such circumstances. This shows the fallacy of singling out a particular boat which does very well and arguing that the rating rule should be changed to penalize those features which are thought to give her an advantage. As for so-called

unseaworthy boats and those that fall to pieces, it does not require a rating rule to develop boats like this. There are plenty of boats which are unseaworthy which are not designed to the IOR and some which are not even permitted to be measured to it.

The IOR has been the first rating rule to which yachts have raced around the world and in myriad events of a punishing nature. There are some bad designers, bad builders and unwise owners who have competed in poor boats, but the rule is not guilty. However as for the dual purpose boat, one owner of a 30 footer wrote to a national newspaper in England which had published criticisms of the IOR 'it is simply not true that the IOR has produced unseaworthy boats that are difficult to sail. Many so called cruising designs are so overweight and have such poor windward ability that sailing them is a doubtful pleasure and comes near to being dangerous under some conditions. Comment has also been made that the provision of adequate accommodation is incompatible with competitiveness. This again is unsupported by the evidence. My own boat sleeps four in greater comfort than I have enjoyed in many cruising boats and her crew sleep on her on every occasion she races. She has also provided two family holidays this season. As for competitiveness I can only add that she won all three of the Pimms Level Rating Trophies . . .'.

There is of course obsolescence under the rule. There is obsolescence with all seagoing vessels and indeed other man-made objects. Facetiousness is not intended, however; the real point is the *rate* of obsolescence and this is difficult to pin down because it is compounded by top skippers and crews obtaining and racing new boats. The best crews like to come to a new boat with all that that means in material apart from rating considerations, but for careful observers of the yachting scene in the middle 70's there have been a number of notable cases where designers' repeat efforts have failed to improve the rating/speed position. The owner would have been better with his old yacht. There are new failures and new successes. There are old failures, but only a limited number of old successes because that is not the way the top owners like to play the game. But there is obsolescence and that is why there are systems which include age allowance and the new retrospective rating rule (page 155).

The matter of fashion, or perhaps more accurately the racing techniques of the moment, should not be overlooked. At any time rigs may be getting larger, sterns wider, keels deeper, centre-boards more frequent, beam narrower as owners and designers find some acknowledged norm which they believe is the way to success. Such trends move first one way and then the other over the years and it would be a mistake for the rule makers to 'chase them' rather than let them 'run out of steam'.

The point should also not be forgotten that, as stated earlier in this book, the rating figure of a particular yacht is a very personal thing. The owner may not be able to change the course which is set, the time allowance system in use and certainly not the weather. But he can fill in a form, after making some alteration on his boat, to bring along the measurer in the expectation of a lower rating. Of course, this is only the other side of the coin to making alterations on the boat so that she will go faster. Such alterations may cause the rating to go up or down, but the owner hopes that the alteration in respect of rating will be advantageous. This, too, is the way the game is played.

## Running the rule

The international body has no option but to run what is often called 'a building rule'. The rule may be based historically on formulae which were intended to rate a variety of existing yachts, but the fact today is that the majority of the fleet were built to the IOR and will continue to be so. Attempts to change the rule to equate a wide variety at this stage would, as already explained, only result in new rule beaters. The ITC is therefore right to work piecemeal in closing loopholes, which are mainly measurement evasions and uncertain definitions. It would be a disaster to go for the 'utopian' solution which would scrap the IOR Mark III and start again with some simple formula based on what is thought to be the causes of yacht performance. There are, of course, the proponents of the 'orange box' rule. This says that a rule should reflect every single speed producing factor so that the latest slick machine would have no advantage over the oldest and roughest ketch: the handicap would equate them if both crews raced their boats at theoretical best. The mathematics of such a rule would be the equivalent of towing each of these yachts in theoretical ideal conditions and finding their resistance (and driving power). One critic said that such a system would enable designers to design boats that they really wanted to, rather than be constricted by the rule. The answer is there would certainly be some shocking boats about and no incentive whatsoever to have a yacht of reasonable performance.

On the question of 'variety', the council

| Date | Change made or rejected |
|------|------------------------|
| April 1971 | Extra mid depths instituted |
| | Strut required for exposed shaft |
| | 'Joke' sail under main boom prohibited |
| November 1971 | IOR Mark III introduced with modifications to L, D, S and CGF. Centreboards defined to prevent swivel keels. Movable appendage factor introduced for centreboards etc. CGF minimum laid down. |
| April 1972 | Blooper declared legal |
| November 1972 | Measures against cat ketches. |
| | Tankage rules for measurement revised. Liferaft at time of measurement clarified. |
| April 1973 | Propeller pitch defined for types of blade. Adjustable leech lines banned in spinnakers. |
| April 1974 | Changes to rule on outboard motors, sheer line, bulbous bows, bloopers, bumps at depth stations. Prevention on use of micro-balloon rejected. |
| November 1974 | Outboard platforms carrying stanchions prohibited, blooper again defined, trim and stowage rules tightened. |
| | Limiting number of sails discussed, new measurement trim proposals rejected. |
| April 1975 | Change in MR to penalize sail area rejected. USYRU proposals on measurement trim rejected. Limiting number of sails not agreed by council. Life raft to be put ashore at measurement. |
| November 1975 | IOR Mark IIIA (retrospective rating introduced) |
| November 1976 | Changes in stern measurement, allowances granted for strut drive propellers. Number of sails limited. |

*Fig 33. Corrections made to the IOR between 1971–1976. There have been many smaller ones mainly dealing with measurement correction and several ideas which have been floated and rejected without being formally recorded. This is one answer to those who accuse the IOR of being a static rule.*

is right not to be hypnotized by this term. The rule only deals with a certain sort of yacht. For instance three masted yachts and multihulls are excluded and there is a framework in which boats can be designed and built. These boats are of the IOR class and the similarity between them makes for good racing, though, as we have seen, that similarity is a matter of degree.

As for the complexity of the rule, the answer to this is in historical precedent. The Victorian yachtsmen at one stage debated fiercely whether their rating rule should be a sail area rule, a displacement rule or a length rule. Only the far sighted among them saw that it had to be all three and many other things besides. That the rule critics are at loggerheads themselves is worth mentioning here.

165

For instance there are those who call for a simple rule while there are others that demand that such things as wetted surface should be brought in to make the rule more accurate.

The rule is complex and indeed it must be admitted that at times it is clumsy because of its historic and piecemeal construction. (Fig 33.) But a computer makes short work of such complexity and the many checks and balances make it difficult for a designer to find an obvious loophole at this stage in its evolution. Inelegant it may be, but work it does.

The whole question of a rule committee being aware of this 'drift in design' is very relevant. There will be a tendency

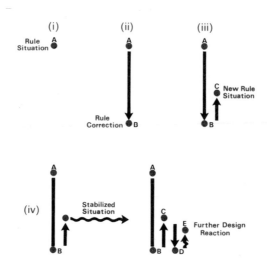

*Fig 34. One system for running a rating rule. Rule makers should accept that if they aim for a 'desirable boat' it will never be quite what they expect. The point of stability must be allowed to find its own level. (i) Situation of rule which requires correction as in (ii). In (iii) the designer reacts to give a new rule situation. (iv) shows alternative actions by a rule committee. It can leave (iii), so stabilizing or go through what is the same process again.*

for certain features to appear to give more and more advantage in one direc- direction, but the writer's practice as chairman of the ITC has been to avoid panic at such points. It is far more satisfactory when such tendencies find their limit or go beyond it.

When a change is made it might be thought of as moving the design so many pegs more in a certain direction. A wise rule-maker knows that the yacht designer will push this back a quarter of the way again. (Fig 34.) It is better to accept this and arrive at a stabilizing point in design rather than make yet a further alteration to the rule to push the design those few pegs back again. This is just one way of looking at procedures of rule changing.

One important consideration in a rule change is whether a re-measurement is required or if the change can be effected by recomputing the certificate from measured data. The policy since the costly introduction of IOR Mark III has been to avoid re-measurement, though there is an intermediate step, whereby additional measurements may be taken on new yachts, or when yachts come up for re-measurement. This is very often the case where the rule change in practice affects only a few yachts and is a 'caution- ary' limitation for the rest. It could be a mark against the administration of the rule that there is an aversion to re- measuring because of the vast number of yachts involved. It is true that there is this retarding effect of the existing fleet. A further retarding effect could be the desire not to upset the level rating classes: in other words, not to introduce rule changes which send some level rated yachts 'over the top' and others below. However ITC policy has been not to be influenced by this possibility. In chapter 16 it was mentioned that level rating figures could be altered in the event of a rule change.

One exercise in support of rule change proposals by critics is often to take existing race results and show how much 'fairer' they would have been had a proposed new formula been applied to the boats in the race. Indeed this can quite readily be shown over a series of races and the argument looks strong. Yet once again if the rule is changed to give such races 'better' results, there is no doubt that yachts would be altered to change their ratings and additionally new boats built to the new rule whatever it might be. Both expensive exercises would help nobody, except perhaps some design offices and boatyards.

Indeed one leading designer who has put considerable work into producing effective boats under the IOR expressed confidence both ways. He said 'I have invested a lot in the IOR and want to go on designing yachts to the rule. But if you guys are going to bring in a different rating rule that's just fine with me. Just as soon as you can let us have the formula, we'll get working on a boat that will win under it . . .'.

# 21. Bibliography

## Periodicals
The following English language magazines contain articles and news on offshore racing.

*Sail*, Boston, Mass.
*Yachting*, New York
*Yacht Racing*, Darien, Conn.
*Soundings*, Essex, Conn.
*Yachting World*, London
*Yachts and Yachting*, London
*Seahorse*, London (Specialist Offshore racing) sponsored by RORC
*Modern Boating*, Sydney
*Australian Seacraft*, Sydney
*Australian Seaspray*, Sydney
*Offshore*, Sydney (Specialist offshore racing) sponsored by CYA
*Canadian Boating*, Toronto
*Sea Spray*, Auckland
*South African Yachting*, Cape Town

## Official publications
USA: United States Yacht Racing Union, P.O. Box 209, Newport, RI 02840 issues IOR Mark III, IYRU rules, Time allowance tables, Portsmouth Yardstick and numbers, special regulations and other publications. Send for list. Rules amendments in regular bulletin to members of USYRU
UK: ORC publications (see Chapter 1) issued direct from ORC office in London. Enquire about Rule amendments sent regularly by direct mail.

Portsmouth Yardstick and numbers and IYRU rules with RYA prescriptions from RYA, Victoria Way, Woking, Surrey, GU21 1EQ
Yacht rating list (UK measured), TMF against ratings. From RORC Rating Office, Station Street, Lymington, Hampshire, SO4 9BA
Similar official publications in other countries: apply to the national authority.

International racing rules, IYRU year book and other publications from IYRU, 60 Knightsbridge, London SW1X 7JX, England.

**Books** *on offshore racing* (with latest edition dates) (Most published both in Britain and USA)

### General
Ocean Racing and Offshore Yachts—Peter Johnson (1972)
The Offshore Racer—Ted Jones (1974) (Emphasis on crew and handling)

### Design
Sailing Yacht Design—D. Phillips-Birt (1976) (Basically sound but based on 1960s practice)
The Way of a Yacht—Alan Hollingsworth (1974) (influences on modern design)
Guinness Book of Yachting Facts and Feats—Peter Johnson (1975) (Includes

history and evolution of yacht design, records of offshore events)
Skenes Elements of Yacht Design— (1974) (Primer, revised, though much old material)

## Crewing
Crewing offshore—Alan Hollingsworth (1965)
Crewing for Offshore Racing—Jeremy Howard-Williams (1973)
(Very sound, but inevitably latest gear not included e.g. nothing on grooved stays)

## History
Ocean Racing—Alf Loomis (US)
British Ocean Racing—D. Phillips-Birt
(Both out of print but basic works on origins of offshore racing)
Ocean racing around the world—Antrobus, Hammond and Ross

## Weather
Heavy weather sailing—K. Adlard Coles (1975) (Essential reading)
Instant weather forecasting—Alan Watts (1968)
Instant wind forecasting—Alan Watts (1976)
(Both based on colour photographs)

## Sails
Sail Power—Wally Ross (1975)
Sails—Jeremy Howard-Williams (1976)

**Navigation** (numerous books, but the following still win on brevity and offshore racing attitudes)
Navigation for Yachtsmen—Mary Blewitt (1973)
Celestial Navigation for Yachtsmen— Mary Blewitt (1975)

# Index

DISTRESS SIGNALS   57–59
DISTRESS BY RADIO   102, 106
EMERGENCY EQUIPMENT STOWAGE   70
MAN OVERBOARD   75
FIRST AID   110
RESUSCITATION AND ARTIFICIAL RESPIRATION   114–115
FOG SIGNALS   52
ORC SPECIAL REGULATIONS FOR SAFETY AND
EMERGENCY EQUIPMENT   60

## index